ARTIST AS HEALER

Stories of Transformation and Healing

NINA AYIN REIMER

NOVELWEAVER PRESS

ARTIST AS HEALER
Stories of Transformation and Healing

Second edition
© Copyright 2021 Nina Ayin Reimer

ISBN: 978-0-9742339-4-9

Library of Congress Number: 2021915290
1. Stories2. Art, Doll-making, Creativity 3. Healing

First edition published 2003
ISBN 0-9472339-0-0

Exceptions to this copyright:
Special thanks to Hilda Ward for permission to reprint her poem,
"Sit Quietly and Take it in"
Quote by Cynthia Ozick

Book design: Jo-Anne Rosen

Nina Reimer, Publisher
Dolls For The Soul/ NovelWeaver Press
dollsforthesoul@usa.net
Manufactured in the United States

In Memory

Uzuri Amini was a doll-maker, writer/ poet,
ceremonialist and priest in the Ifa spiritual tradition of
the Yoruban People of West Africa. Her light in spirit
remains strong with all of us who loved her.

For my parents and ancestors
who guide me from a place of Light.
For my nephew, Tyler and my many departed loved ones
whose spirits are always with me.

When you sit quietly and allow yourself to hear your heart
Then your soul can come forth to comfort you
When you sit quietly and listen to the wind and feel the flowers
Then your soul takes on the contentment it begs for
When you sit quietly and view the vastness of the mountains
Then your soul can feel the presence of its Divine Creator
When you sit quietly and view the tiny creatures of the earth
Then your soul can feel deep into the soil of life
When you sit quietly and feel the flow of the wings above
Then your soul can step out and fly with a joy
When you sit quietly and feel the mist of the waves
Then your soul can be washed clean with a pureness
When you sit quietly and watch a deer slide gracefully in your path
Then your soul can feel the gentle love of your Higher Power
When you sit quietly and feel the earth under your feet
Then your soul can plant itself solid in your temple…

—Excerpt from "Sit Quietly and Take It In"

by Hilda Ward, grandmother, great grandmother. poet and author of *Pieces of Her African American Quilt*, *Love Nickles* (Gifts From Our Grandmothers); CD titles, "Images" and "Oh! How I Praise Thee!"

Contents

Preface

"To imagine the unimaginable is the highest use of the imagination."

— Cynthia Ozick

Dolls have contributed to the cultures of nations from Asia to Africa, from Europe to the Americas for centuries. Dolls have been unearthed within tombs of ancient Greece, Rome, and Egypt. Dolls of India provide a unique illustration of 5,000 years of Indian civilization. Native American cultures, as well, have a long history of doll making.

Whether created for use as toys, spiritual objects, for teaching socialization or for therapeutic purposes, dolls have made an impact on the lives of the people around them. Utilizing stone, cloth, wood, clay and even vegetables, doll makers have sought to give life to the images of the humans around them or to express some inner being who sought life through the maker's hands.

Children have spent countless hours on adventures with their unique companions thus developing their imagination and intellect. Adults have used dolls to emphasize some area of their lives such as women in some indigenous tribes of Africa who carry dolls around on their waists to bring or represent fertility.

As a doll maker myself, I was moved by the intricate nature of Nina's remarkable dolls, when I met her some years ago. After getting to know Nina, I had the experience of receiving a doll from her and making a number of dolls with her guidance. I discovered the deep level from which she worked and the serious nature of the healing ability of her dolls.

It was after I attended one of her workshops, that I was guided by my own spiritual tradition to make two dolls for my Ancestors-one for my matriarchal line and one for my patriarchal line. Nina helped me to connect to my Ancestors, create and complete this task with such respect and care that my Ancestors and I thank her daily.

As we worked together, I found that Nina's gift goes beyond the usual boundaries of doll-making. Her work both informs the inner person as it helps the conscious mind to grow. Whether she makes the doll or you create a doll with her help, the connection between the psyche, spirit, and body is consistently apparent. Through Nina's work, I have discovered the ability of a doll to bring not only comfort, but also insight and change. Manifested through the dolls' presence I have experienced her dolls' emotional and spiritual healing power.

These are the stories of an extraordinary healing artist.

Read, enjoy and savor them!

Uzuir Amini, 2003

Acknowledgments

Through the years of learning my art,
I wish to thank so many who stood by my side—
Diana, for your insight and encouragement,
my son for your courage, wisdom, and humor,
and all my family for your generosity and Love.

To my friends and students at the
International Women's Writing Guild
who have I have been honored to know
and who have been my teachers all along.

And especially Jerry,
for helping me to remember....

ARTIST AS HEALER

Stories of Transformation and Healing

Introduction

For years, I have been telling stories of my life and my journey as an artist and healer. In person, the storytelling is joyful, funny, sad, poignant and ultimately—spiritually renewing. In front of an audience, I can observe and appreciate those moved to laughter and tears by these stories of transformation and healing.

Now for the first time, I have written some of the stories. For you, the reader, the essence of this medium may alter the flavor of the stories. Nonetheless, it is my intent to share with you a glimpse of what is possible—how the ordinary may, in fact, *be the extraordinary*.

I always tell my audiences, that I am no different than any one of you. I say this, because I believe that we all have the power to heighten our awareness, our intuitive side. Given time, energy and focus—psychic awareness is possible for most human beings. The chance to see new meaning in life, to find answers, to seek truth and to heal ourselves and the earth, is within our collective grasp.

But most of us are too busy going about what we consider our ordinary lives to devote much time and energy to fertilizing our intuition or our *higher spiritual self*. We may be too distracted, stressed, or burdened with responsibilities to give our spiritual side–our soul the attention it needs. Maybe, we attend religious services and believe strongly that this is the totality of a nurturing spiritual life. Maybe we are at demanding jobs, even creative jobs, helping others all day, tending to the environment, social issues or family concerns. We put aside our own creative endeavors for later...always later, because we see creativity as a luxury, a hobby or something beyond our ability. We may not recognize it as spiritual or healing. We may not accept creativity as a necessity for feeding our spirit the same way we acknowledge the body's need for sustenance.

Often, we are just too committed to *time*, as we perceive it in the material, physical world—and to its demands. We consciously refuse to give up any of it or "waste time" on anything other than that which we have come to trust as concrete, traditional, factual, or scientific. We rarely step beyond the boundaries we have created or that we have allowed to be created for us. We forget or do not truly believe in any reality other than the one in which "time" controls us.

Our popular belief that science and spirituality are opposites, reinforce the polarity between real work and art. Thus, we are often thwarted from taking the risks required to be true to our (higher) selves. In doing so, we deny ourselves an opportunity to evolve, heal and experience miracles.

Often, it is fear that drives us, motivates us, or anchors us to a dense version of ourselves as non-evolving creatures. I spent many years of my life allowing fear to prevent me from understanding the connection between spirituality, creativity and healing. I considered my spiritual growth to be the time I devoted to celebrating religious traditions and holidays. As a young adult, I felt conflicted in creating art when concerns for social justice drew my attention. Later, I viewed making art as a luxury I could not afford, unless it was in pursuit of making a living. Making great art was not something for which women were expected to strive, so I felt that I needed to be practical. I was afraid to live as an artist—afraid of poverty, ridicule and others' expectations. I tried for many years to ignore my creative side, not realizing how my spirit suffered. Depression, lack of energy and frustration became my companions, but I did not make the connection for a long time.

Now, if young people I meet express the desire to be poets, photographers, musicians, painters... I say, "*Go for it...Follow your heart and spirit!*" It will be these children (and other creative young people) that bring healing, light and peace to our world, if we can get out of the way and let them. It is imperative to our survival that we continue to paint, to write, to sing, to sculpt... a world in which the artist in all of us survives and thrives! It is through creativity that we enable ourselves to override the messages of fear.

It is through creativity that we express self-love, learn to heal ourselves and discover our soul's essence in joy. During the meditative state of creativity, Spirit speaks through us. Who has listened to beautiful music and not felt a stirring in their heart, in their soul? In the face of such Light, fear loosens its grip. It is through the creative element that universal love, humor, compassion and passion for life—flourish.

I often tell audiences that, in the creative work I do, I listen to Guidance. People will ask, "Do you hear voices?" *Fear* exists within this question. Because traditional Western medicine tells us that "hearing voices" is not normal and is a part of mental illness, we are afraid, skeptical. Barely given consideration in such circles (although, more so lately) are psychics, for whom such phenomenon is neither uncommon nor a sign of illness.

In cultures around the world, and including our Native American traditions, speaking *with* spirits of our ancestors, animals, deities or God, does not equate to mind illness. Shamans or Elders in tribal societies often use spiritual communication to heal. However, with the exclusion of mysticism, conformity to traditional Judeo-Christian practices does not allow for much diversion, so communication with such things as animal spirits is often deemed mythology, at best. For many of us, it is okay to pray to (speak to) Our Father/ God, but it is suspect, if anyone answers.

Thus, many people are *fearful* of developing their own intuitive side. They may be afraid others will think them weird or crazy. They may be confined by constricted belief systems or just afraid that such exploration may cause them isolation, lack of love, ostracization. It is an interesting phenomenon that people are often pushed beyond their fear, to question deeper understanding of spirituality, in the face of death. As people face death, which is a frightening concept for many, they are more open to consider or accept other realities. So, it is *fear* that is the real issue for many.

Fear acts as an entity. Fear has a chemical effect on the body, as do other emotions. As instinct, fear has a helpful role as a warning system to keep the body physically safe. Fearful thoughts can, however, distort the response to stimuli as well negatively impact the body's aura and vibrational energy. A person suffering from a mind disorder or stress-related breakdown is often in a state of agitation—panic or fear is often both a contributing factor and a result of *uncontrollable* auditory or visual stimuli. The common reaction to a person whose visual or auditory perceptions may be "out of control" (from chemical imbalance, brain injury of any other cause), is usually fear and efforts at control. It is natural, given the latter scenario, that fear may prevent us from acknowledging any heightened intuitive side we have begun to develop. Sometimes in developing heightened intuition the initial stages of psychic evolution may mimic mental instability. Because we have been taught to fear that which we cannot see, the first encounters with heightened intuition in an auditory form (whether spontaneous or consciously attained through a meditative state) may make one feel frightened. In a supportive environment or in cultures that support multi-dimensional realities one does not experience fear, but often elation, acceptance and peace associated with *unconditional love*. For those who practice traditional religions, but whose belief in angels, life after death and/or reincarnation is accepted, there is considerably less fear of heightened intuition, as well.

Dialogue about our experiences is vital to expose the myths, promote understanding and create a supportive environment based on truth. For those who need "proof" and equate only science with truth—more evidence will be coming in the very near future.

Those who do embrace their own heightened intuition, while not all alike in ability, do have the capacity to use their *conscious release of control* to help others. It is a lack of fear, self-acceptance of intuitive sensitivity, and the conscious release of control that gives psychics a positive vibrational pathway to receive visual and auditory information. Through an acceptance of love, prayer, meditation and/or affirmations, intuitive healers, for example, work to restore the body and mind to its natural, positive vibration and to access helpful information.

Lack of fear, however, is not simply the absence of fear. It is the acceptance of Fear as a teacher of negative energy and the acceptance of Love as truth or positive universal energy...call it Spirit, God, Goddess or Divine Love.

Being a psychic, an intuitive or shaman does not exclude one from the human condition. Conversely, it is not only such people who are "born with special gifts"—we all have the potential to be a part of *knowing* our reality. It is through *practice of our individual creative gifts—which we all have—* that we arrive at the threshold of knowing. It is up to each one of us to *remember* our soul's purpose and to embrace our individual *creative capacity* in order to bring forth that which we most desire...love, peace, health, and abundance for ourselves and our world.

Each one of us plays a part. Each one of us is a mirror and a teacher. The reflections and lessons are all around us, all of the time. Think about each time, just before the phone rings, how we anticipate the call; each time we have a hunch, a premonition or dream that comes true; each time we think something is a coincidence; any time we are spared harm, when by all accounts, we should not be okay; each time we meet someone for the first time who seems so familiar, we think we must have met that person before; each time communication takes place between us and the pet we cherish; each time we create something of beauty or do something that changes someone's life for the better... These are just some doorways and signposts...tiny clues on our path.

I am learning—still gathering clues and so I offer you these stories. It is often said, "truth is stranger than fiction." Some people may not believe that the stories within these pages are true, but they are. I have written them as they happened, only changing some names, dates or settings for the sake of privacy.

This book is about *creativity, healing and transformation.* I feel blessed to be able to share *my* journey, *Artist As Healer,* with you—in hope that it will lighten and enlighten your own.

Nina Ayin Reimer

*In every lifetime there comes a moment that if realized,
changes and elevates consciousness, our closeness to each other
and to the oneness of creation. Taking the risk to see, hear
and accept the truth—no matter what face it wears—is to
begin a journey of transformation.*

*One day, in the spring of 1993, I turned down a strange
road. I took that risk and leaped into the unknown. These are
true stories of what transpired.*

Meeting Mrs. Saxon

I pulled up to the curb at the edge of the straggly, overgrown front lawn of 301 Montpelier Lane. A small gray-shingled house stood a few hundred feet back from the road. It was similar to the rest of the homes in the neighborhood except it looked older, perhaps because of the large maple trees on the front lawn.

I looked at the clock on the dashboard. It was exactly 3:00 pm. The new student I was about to meet should have been home from school for half an hour by now, I thought. I would make a good impression on him and his mom by being so punctual. I set the car's brake, then checked for my glasses in the briefcase I'd filled with notebooks and assessment materials.

Having the supplies I needed, I felt confident as I walked up the slate path overgrown with crabgrass. When I reached the front steps, I noticed a fresh pot of yellow mums and a very large pink quartz crystal on the landing. They offered an unusual and alluring quality to the otherwise unkempt exterior of this small drab house. I looked along the doorframe for the doorbell. Not finding one, I reached for the tarnished brass knocker attached to the solid front door. I tapped gingerly and waited.

Moments ticked by with no answer. So I knocked again, this time harder. Still, there was no answer. I was about to knock for the last time before leaving, when the door opened. A frail woman in dark pants and a blue wool cardigan peered from the opening. She was whisper thin. Her hair was drab gray, like her house and like the weather that day. Her eyes, though, were a cool penetrating light blue. She held the ends of her sweater closed with one hand around her thin and clearly chilled frame. "Oh," she finally said, "come in, come in...I've been expecting you. I'm Toni Saxon. Just call me Toni. Have you been waiting long? "

"No, not long. I knocked..."

"Yes, the bell broke a while ago. I don't hear when someone knocks sometimes... would you like a cup of coffee? It's damp and chilly out there today, isn't it?"

"Yes, it is," I responded politely. It was colder than usual for early October. The offer of a hot cup of coffee sounded great, but I didn't want to waste any more time. I was anxious to meet the child. Maybe her grandchild, I now reconsidered. "Is Timmy here?" I inquired.

"My son, Timmy is not home yet. I mean he went out to play for a while, but I told him to come back soon...as soon as he saw a car drive up. He is next door at the neighbor's house, playing. Come in and have some coffee...he'll be back soon," she said, as she led the way up three steps to what one might call a living room. It was dark. A bit of light filtered in through the half-drawn blinds. There was enough light to see that the room was devoid of furniture. Boxes lined the edge of the room and a glass and wood cabinet with dishes in it, stood against the wall near the fireplace. Perhaps they had recently moved in, I thought.

"Excuse my house. My furniture is elsewhere temporarily. We are thinking about painting this room." Toni talked as she moved. It did briefly pass my consciousness that she seemed to be responding to my thoughts, as I'd said very little. I was in first impression, observer mode.

Soon we were in the kitchen, which by contrast was bright and airy. Although cluttered, it had clearly been redecorated. It was more contemporary with a glass windowed porch adjacent to the small dining area. The windows looked out on a wooded lot where large birch and pine trees obscured the view of the house next door. I relaxed a little.

"Please sit." Toni pointed to a chair at the kitchen table, then pulled two cups and saucers from a cupboard over the sink. A fresh pot of coffee sat in the lap of the coffee maker on the counter. Toni filled each cup. "Cream and sugar?" she asked placing a steaming cup in front of me.

"Yes, thank you," I said. I was drawn to the rich aroma like any devoted caffeine addict. Besides, a few more minutes wouldn't matter I rationalized. After all, her child was not there.

Although the child's absence did seem odd, I let the ambiance of the kitchen with its windows on the natural world and the sweet warm coffee soothe me, momentarily. I watched Toni as she moved toward the table with her cup in hand. She had seen the flyer about my tutoring and had called me about her nine year-old son, who was having difficulty with reading. That was my specialty. I'd talked to her by phone, but this was the first time we were meeting. I had not imagined her to look so old.

Toni sat down with her coffee, across the table from me. "You know," she began, "I'm glad you're here. I've been expecting you."

"Uh...yes," I said hesitating. What did she mean by that? Of course, she would be expecting me. We'd made an appointment by phone...unless...suddenly, I realized that maybe she didn't remember that we had had a conversation about tutoring her son. Maybe, she thought I was someone else. Maybe, she had hired another tutor or someone to talk to about her son.

"Yes, I'm Ayin," I said. "We spoke by phone about..."

"Yes, yes...I've been expecting you," she repeated getting up from her chair. "Wait here, I've got to go to the basement. I'll be right back. More coffee?" She seemed to be next to me refilling my cup before I could respond. Then, Toni placed the pot on the counter and hurried out of the kitchen.

I squirmed in the chair. Time was going by. There was no child around to tutor. Toni Saxon seemed just a bit strange and now I was sitting in her house drinking coffee and not knowing whether I would even be paid for my time. I should just leave, I thought. I could drink coffee in my own kitchen, while I observed my own child's homework progress. I needed to work. I would explain to Toni again that I tutored professionally. This was not a visit. I started to get up from the chair as I took the last sip of coffee. I would tell Toni when she came back to the kitchen that I needed to leave and thank her for the coffee. I would explain how I ran my business; how I made a living tutoring on a hourly basis; how I handled missed appointments; that my time was valuable and I could not afford to...

"You see, Ayin..." Toni appeared as if out of nowhere. She was standing before me cradling something in her arms. "You see, my Dear," she said yet again, this time slower, more deliberately. "I've been expecting you." I looked in her eyes then down at the object in her arms.

Slowly, she turned around what appeared to be a small doll. I stared at it.

Suddenly, time seemed to shift, to slow down and the air seemed to vibrate. I was aware of my own voice, only it seemed far away. I could hear myself talking as if under water.

"That doll looks just like me, doesn't it?" I said feeling the words in my throat. My eyes were riveted on the doll, as chills danced up my spine. Then, tears came. I choked them back. I stared at this doll with a face like a mirror image of me, looking into my soul, dressed in robes and braids. I could find no words for the emotions. Lack of verbiage was not normally one of my attributes.

I looked at the frail woman in front of me. She looked totally different. Her eyes shown and twinkled brightly. A flush filled her cheeks turning her formerly sallow skin a rosy pink. Had she somehow magically transformed into a younger, vibrant version of herself before my eyes? Before I could fully register what was happening, she placed the doll in my arms and disappeared again down to the basement.

"Wait here..." her voice trailed off. I waited transfixed, immobilized. But I must have glanced out the windows for an instant, because I remember hearing the sound of laughter coming from that direction. The trees were dancing wildly in what seemed a suddenly strong wind and I could have sworn I heard them laughing! Oh, how could that be...I was thinking, when Toni appeared without making a sound, just as she had before.

This time she carried a larger doll in her hands. She placed him on the table. I could not stop the gasp that rose from the pit of my stomach, it seemed. There, before me, was a doll portrait of my great uncle...the one whose father had been killed by wolves in the forests of Russia. My own father had told us the story. He had only one picture of this man and his family. It was such an unusual picture of my old Mongolian family heritage, that I cherished it. There was no mistaking this portrait, or the exact same traditional clothes. "How? What?" I began to speak, but found I could not formulate a sentence coherently.

"You see, Ayin, this is no accident that you came here today. I have been expecting you. They told me you would come."

"They?" I managed to blurt out. No, not again I thought. I'd heard about "they" before. I didn't want any part of "they". From the time I was a small child "they" had had power over life and death. "They", the fascists, the racists, the enemy. Then "they", the demons and spirits. Now "they", the watchers, the others, the guardians, the undead, the angels. I'd heard enough about "they" to last a lifetime. A few years ago, after a "paranormal" experience, I moved and started over. I would not open that door again—not again.

I felt the adrenaline rush and my body said, "rise, run... run out of here!" But the air was heavy and swirling about me. I could not feel my body. It was as if all my atoms were in disarray. I sat in my chair, a captive audience bound by invisible rope. Had there been something in the coffee? I felt drugged. But it wasn't a sluggish, happy feeling. It was a tingling, vibrating feeling. I felt alive, a part of the air, connected to every atom in the room. Yet I could not bring myself to move in spite of the fear I felt.

"Don't be afraid," a deep voice said. I looked at Toni Saxon. Her lips were moving, but her voice was not her own, not the one with which she had offered me coffee.

"You can't run away from your own truth, anymore, Ayin," her new voice said. "You must do the work. This is your path. There is no more time. Now, Ayin, you must begin. I will show you the way without fear. You do not have a choice. The time has come. Take this doll and it will open the door." Toni was suddenly standing close to me placing my doll-likeness in my arms. "Do not be afraid. Look at this doll." I followed the voice's command. Tears welled up in my eyes again as I looked at the warm little wise one in my hands. "She is you, Ayin. Stop what you are doing. You must begin your real work now."

I felt suspended. Somewhere my heart pounded. Toni Saxon turned away and began puttering in some cupboards. When she turned around, she was herself again. "I think I hear Timmy coming," she said. Her voice had returned to it normal pitch.

I heard myself laughing loudly. I no longer believed there was a Timmy. And I didn't hear anything. It was all a joke! With my sense of humor back, my body entered real time and the air returned to normal.

"Hi, Mom!" A boy appeared suddenly at the kitchen entrance. He was muddy and sweaty, like he'd been sliding into home base or dirt biking. "Oh!" he said covering his mouth with a dirty hand when he saw me at the kitchen table.

"Where have you been? I told you the tutor was coming!" Toni tried to control her aggravation. "Wash up, you're a mess." She turned to me. "I'm sorry," she said. "He never listens."

"It's okay," I said stunned by the boy's existence. Timmy turned and walked down the hall to the bathroom. I turned my attention back to Toni. How could she maneuver between worlds so fast? How did one manage to hear voices of another realm and live a normal, dirty child, dirty dishes, homework kind of existence, switching back and forth like a faucet, without losing one's mind. I'd had the unfortunate familiarity with such an experience once and I wanted no part of it. Please just let me tutor this kid and be normal, I thought.

But it was too late for that, obviously. I was not normal. Hadn't everyone always told me so? Wasn't my family's mantra: "What the hell's the matter with you?" Having lived through hell once I didn't relish going they're again. But, maybe this would be different. Maybe this time, I'd meet up face to face with the "theys" and give them a piece of my mind. I'd tell them to speak loud and clear to me directly, and not leave messages for me with everybody else.

A memory flashed before me. I was ten. Everyday for some years I'd walk the long, slow road home after school and somewhere along the way "they" would start, softly—then suddenly louder, calling my name. "Ayin... Ayin...AYIN!" I'd be sure someone was behind me and I'd turn around, each time positive I'd find the person— some nasty little boy playing a trick on me, hiding behind some tree, calling and calling my name. Many years later, when I had willed the "theys" away, friends would tell me of messages they had received for me in their dreams—messages which had awakened them from sleep and terrified them.

Suddenly, Toni Saxon's words made sense. I'd been running away a very long time. It was time to stop. It was time to listen. But, I was still so scared.

"Ayin, why don't you come back on Wednesday to see Timmy. I'll be sure he is ready for you next time. I'll pay you for the two days this week. I'm sorry he was so late." She walked over toward me. She picked up my little doll-like image that I had placed back on the table and tucked it in my arms again. Her voice resumed its trance-like tone and instructions poured forth into my ear. She put one arm around my shoulder and soon she was escorting me to my car with this doll, all the while repeating the instructions and encouraging me to return.

I remember having a hard time breathing and seeing the road beyond the tears that streamed down my face. I was not usually a crier. I wiped the tears away before I got to my own place. I knew my own child would be home from school and trusted that he was the most rational, down to earth person I knew. He would know that all of this was just my imagination and that this doll did not look like me at all. He was my lifeline, my rock. Life would be normal again in just a few minutes.

I got out of the car, walked up the steps and into the house. Michael, my eighth grader, a kid growing into his adolescence, was watching after-school TV. "Hi, Mom... what's wrong? Are you sick? You look white as a ghost!"

"Hi to you to, honey. No, I'm okay, just tired. I'm going to..."

"What's that?" Michael said, noticing the doll tucked in my arm.

"Uh..." I turned it around so he could see it fully. Surely, it would be nothing he'd be even comment on.

"Wow, Mom, where'd you get that? It looks just like you!"

No, no, NO ! Please say something different, I thought. "You think so? A student's mother made it for me for a present. Isn't that sweet? I'm going to my room to lay down for a little while, dear. I'll make dinner soon. Are you hungry? Did you have something?" I said nervously.

I didn't wait to long for his answer. I went to my room. I looked at the little doll as I laid it next to my pillow. Then I lay down too. I was exhausted. I closed my eyes, but they popped open a second later. Who was I kidding? Sleep would probably turn into a thing of the past. I'd stepped over some invisible boundary and there was no turning back. It was time to wake up. It was time to remember.

Later that evening, with homework, dishes, laundry done and the eleven o'clock news turned off after the weather, I climbed into bed. Michael's bedroom lights were out. The cat and dog were asleep. I climbed into bed and adjusted the little doll next to me as instructed. I turned off my light and nestled into my pillow for a well-deserved sleep. Immediately, a world of symbols, emblems, hieroglyphics, codes and images...languages of a thousand cultures and times exploded all at once inside my head. I tried to open my eyes. I could not. Something held me inside this place where information poured through my pores, my blood, my cells, my mind's eye, faster than humanly comprehensible. My body reacted in fear... fight or flight. I forced myself into an upright position and willed my eyes open. I heard a rush of wind at my ear.

I looked down at this doll next to me. "Oh, shit!" I said. I took her to the closet and set her on a shelf and closed the door. But before I got back to bed, I turned around, put the doll on a lower shelf, facing out toward my bed, and left the closet door ajar, lest I offend "anyone." I got back into bed. My privacy was shattered, once again. I thought about my mother, whose religion was science and history... No wonder she thought I was nuts. Then I recited the 23rd psalm over and over, hoping that sleep or dawn would find me soon.

The Blue Robe

Four months following my first encounter with Mrs. Saxon, I had learned to make little doll figures. She had taken me under her wing and introduced me to a friend who owned a little gallery where she made and sold dolls. As I had been a medical illustrator in my earlier years and had sculpted before, it did not take me very long to craft faces that resembled real people. Mrs. Saxon and her friend were enamored by the reality I brought to my work. I offered to share my anatomical knowledge with them, but each had their own style of work. They had both learned the craft of facial structure through mold making rather than building, so neither seemed as enthralled with the art of sculpting as I was.

The holidays were fast approaching and my tutoring days with Timmy were coming to an end. He had been placed in a new school that had an after school program. I was on my own with my new craft, working at home and in the gallery's studio. I had no idea why I was making doll figures, except that I was having great fun doing a series of what looked like my Eastern European ancestors. I was able to sell one or two of them at the gallery, but I did not ask for much over the cost of materials. My hours at the gallery had increased as the owner devoted more time to a sick relative, so I was making an hourly wage and doing something artistic.

On occasion, I would see Mrs. Saxon and one day I asked her what I was to gain from doing this work? All she said was "When the time comes, you will know what you need to know." When I asked about the dreams I continued to have that were disturbing sometimes, even frightening on occasion, she was succinct. "They are lessons in fear...you need to learn to release fear." And that was all she said.

Then, one day a week before Christmas, I was working at home making dolls as presents for friends when I got a strange feeling about one of the dolls. She was not like any of the others I had made. She was blonde, blue-eyed and had a little straight nose and high cheekbones. Her face was delicate, yet she was middle-aged. I pondered as to what clothing to sew for her as I only had red and green holiday fabrics and wanted something blue to match her bright eyes. I worked until late into the afternoon finishing everything except the clothes.

I was so engrossed that I lost track of time. It was my day off and I had forgotten to go to the market as I had planned. So, I quickly took stock of what was in the cupboards, the freezer and rummaged through what remained in the vegetable drawer of the refrigerator, throwing out old lettuce, a soft zucchini and some less than fresh carrots. Then, I put on my coat, grabbed the now full garbage bag and headed out the door stopping at the trash-can on the side of the garage to toss the bag. I shared the trash area with my next door neighbor as our houses were on joined property. I opened the lid of the can and glanced inside to see if there was room, when I noticed it.

There in the trash, on a bed of clean white plastic, lay what appeared to be a neatly folded blue robe. I put down my bag and carefully picked up the robe. The smell of laundry detergent lingered in its folds of soft velour. The only tell-tale sign of use was the faded piping at the collar. I traded the garbage for the robe and went back into the house. I hung the robe near the washing machine. I would launder it one more time after dinner. Then, I resumed my path to the market, gleeful at my good luck. Blue velour had not been in my sparse budget for the holiday season, since my son's presents and a holiday dinner took precedence. A joyous mood followed me through dinner. I even offered to do my son's clean-up chores after dinner, so I could get right back to work on the dining room table while he did his homework.

That evening, I pulled the beautiful robe from the dryer and cut it into a pattern to make a flowing robe for the little blue-eyed doll. She would look just beaming in this luscious fabric. As I fitted her robe I had the oddest feeling. Suddenly, I realized that this doll must go to my neighbor. It must have been her robe and must return to her, was what registered in my mind.

I finished the doll, putting all kinds of things in her hands—some coins, a bit of herbs and a tiny heart-shaped locket. I watched myself as if from afar choosing these things, but not knowing why. When the doll was finished though, she looked dazzling. I placed her in a brightly colored holiday shopping bag in my hall closet with all the other presents I had made.

The day before Christmas was very cold and gray. I woke early. I showered and dressed before my son was even awake. As I drank hot coffee and peered out the kitchen window, I could see the lights come on at my neighbor's house. I decided to bring her the blue-robed doll and without hesitation took it out of the hall closet. I tried to write a "Happy Holidays" note, not really knowing what to say. We had moved into our small house only the past summer, so I did not really know my neighbor very well. I had the fleeting thought that she might not like dolls or think it weird that I was giving her something. But I had this feeling of urgency as well, so I dismissed the negative thoughts. I wrapped my scarf about my neck and zipped my jacket. Out the door, into the morning twilight I went with the doll package in hand.

I knocked on the door twice and soon my neighbor, Ginger, opened the door. She was surprised to see me standing there. I noticed a little holiday figurine on her hall table and felt immediately relieved. "Happy Holidays!" I blurted out handing her the bag.

"You got me something?" she asked with dismay. "I…I didn't get you… I don't have anything for you."

"Oh, don't worry. I made this for you." Ginger looked bewildered as she motioned me to step in, out of the cold. We walked into her warm kitchen and she took her doll out of the bag.

"Oh! Oh my God! She is beautiful!" Ginger exclaimed. "You made this? How did you…"

I watched her expression as she touched and turned the doll. Suddenly, I remembered taking the robe out of the trash. I had taken Ginger's robe, (to whom else could it have belonged?) from the trash and was giving it to her! What if she recognized it? A wave of embarrassment swept over me. I had to explain before she recognized it.

"Uh , I ..uh… Do you recognize this fabric?" I said cautiously. Ginger looked more closely and gasped.

"This is my robe!" she cried. Tears formed at the corners of her eyes. "What do you call this doll?" she half whispered.

"I call it...uh, I call it...a...*Healing Doll*," I said. The words popped out of my mouth without my knowing why or from where the idea arose. By now, Ginger was crying, tears streaming down her face. I felt awful. I had gone too far.

"I'm so sorry." I tried to apologize. "I found the robe and it was such beautiful fabric and so carefully placed in the garbage and I just thought ..."

Ginger motioned me to be quiet as she regained her composure. "You have no idea what you have done, have you?"

"No," I replied. "I never meant..."

"I needed this doll," Ginger said. "I need healing and this robe—my new boyfriend did not like it. He said it was worn and bought me a new one. He asked me to get rid of it. But I did not want to. We had a fight. So I gave in and threw it away. You see," Ginger continued, "my daughter had given me this robe seven years ago when I had almost died. I was awaiting an organ transplant. She bought this robe for me to wear in the hospital to heal in and I did. I loved this robe. You're right, I did not want to throw it away. Thank you. Thank you so much for bringing it back to me—on my healing doll!"

Now, I had a lump in my throat. "Oh, thank you for telling me. I am so glad I found it. I don't think your boyfriend will recognize it, do you?"

"No," she said, her voice steadier now. Her face took on a tranquil yet determined look. "No," she boldly said, "I know he won't."

Love Letters

The experience of making my first *Healing Doll* was overwhelming. I walked home thinking how I was onto something incredible. I remembered Mrs. Saxon's words that I would know what I needed to know when the time came. Little did I know that day, that my first healing was just the beginning of my journey.

I was eager to have another chance at making a *Healing Doll* and I did not have to wait long before the opportunity presented itself. A few weeks after the holidays, I was at the laundromat that I frequented with bedding, which was too heavy for my small washing machine at home. The woman attendant, Martha, was folding clothes. We had chatted about the weather, her job at the laundry, and from time to time—the news droning on the TV set perched on a shelf above the row of washing machines. I waved to her as I walked in and went about my routine with coins and soap powder. Then, I sat down in one of the turquoise plastic chairs near the window. I took from my jacket pocket a plastic sandwich bag containing a piece of clay and a wooden tool, and started sculpting some small hands. I looked up and noticed Martha glance in my direction. We exchanged smiles. Then she walked over to me.

"Are you making a doll?" she asked, peering at my hands. I had told her about learning to make dolls on a laundry day chat some months earlier. I had showed her a picture of one of the dolls I had made for a friend for a birthday present.

"Just practicing making hands...they are the hardest part," I held up a small piece of mitten-shaped clay.

"I'd sure love to have one of your dolls, someday," she said wistfully.

"I can make you one, Martha," I offered.

"Oh, no," she said. "I can't afford it, especially not now with all the medical bills coming. Besides, tomorrow is my last day at work for a while." I noticed how pale she looked. "But the doctor thinks I have a good chance if it's not cancer, so that's good news!" Her face brightened as she shook off the gloom around her.

"Cancer? What is wrong, Martha?" I felt the shock of her words before they reached my ear.

"I have a brain tumor," she said quietly. "Been so dizzy lately. I am going in for surgery in a week, but I just have to rest first, you know. I have a friend, though..." she began to whisper as she leaned closer to me. "He's a psychic and he said it wasn't malignant. Do you believe in psychics?"

"Uh, yes, I guess I do and I certainly hope he is right. God, I'm so sorry. Is there anything I can do? If you'd like a doll, don't worry about money. I can..."

"No, dear, but thank you," she interrupted me. "When I get better, maybe." She patted my arm then walked over to the counter to help a customer that had just come in to pick up his wash and fold order. I could tell by her wobbly gate, she was not well.

Before I left with my freshly laundered bedding that day, I asked Martha for her phone number so I could call to see how she was doing. I was determined to make her a doll before her hospital visit. She had confided in me, not only about her health, but also about her beliefs. So, I took it as a sign. I had always had an observant artist's eye, but I had started to pay closer attention with my ears and heart again.

Back at the gallery's studio the following day, I set to work on Martha's doll sculpture. The face of a sweet and demure old woman appeared out of the clay, as I sculpted. Within the next two days she was assembled and dressed in a white blouse and a pink and gray brocade skirt. At the collar was a cameo brooch, while a small strand of pearls completed her jewelry. She held in her hands a tiny porcelain teapot and cup—very English looking— and some roses tucked into one arm. Over the other arm a soft scarlet blanket rested. Her white hair was styled in a lose knot and she smiled with warm brown eyes.

By late afternoon of the third day, I was putting on the finishing touches. The winter sun was nearing the horizon, turning the light throughout the studio my favorite orange hue, when I suddenly felt a terrible pain. It emanated from inside my chest, in my heart. It was the pain of sadness, of longing. It was an ache so intense that I didn't quite know what to do. I calmed myself and sat quietly. The pain came in waves. Slowly, I became aware of a feeling of longing for a young man. My mind went through an inventory of young men I had known, but nothing seem to fit, except for a young man I had lost during wartime long ago.

"But that was so long ago. I'm not pining anymore," I said aloud to an empty room. I struggled to comprehend the feeling when all at once, I could have sworn I heard a voice say…"It's not you! It's her Aunt. Her Aunt is pining for a young man."

"What? Oh, oh my God, what is happening?" Chills ran up and down my body. Then, I felt relieved and joyful and sad all at the same time. Tears flowed down my checks.

I cried and talked to the air and danced around the studio. Had anyone come in at that moment, they might have thought I was in a drug-induced state. I regained my equilibrium, packed up my little English lady and went home to attempt being a normal mom. I stopped and bought a pizza on the way home.

The next day I called Martha. She was surprised to hear from me, but agreed to see me and gave me her address. I drove over with the little English lady-doll wrapped carefully in a box on the car seat beside me. I rang Martha's bell and waited. Soon, she opened the door. She smiled her usual warm smile. She was dressed in casual clothes and looked as if she had been resting.

"Come in," she said, "I'm glad you called. I could use the company. I just put up a pot of tea…would you like some?"

"Oh, yes, thank you," I said. I put the box down on a kitchen chair and took off my coat. Then I picked the box up again and handed it to Martha.

She gave me a *"you shouldn't have"* look, but was eager and happy to open her present. When the doll emerged though, Martha's mouth dropped open. She stared at the doll, then at me, then back at the doll. Color drained from her already pale skin and her eyes moistened. She did not say anything. I panicked. What had I done to this poor sick woman?

"This is my Aunt." Martha finally said, ever so softly. "My mother's sister who raised us. How did you do this? How? How did you know about the brocade and the brooch and the pearls? Gray and pink were her favorite colors...and her white hair? How is this possible?"

"I don't know," I said, honestly. "It just came out that way." I was as astonished as Martha was by her recognition.

"I seem to have some kind of gift, but I don't really know what it is about. I think if you believe that souls do not die—that maybe they are angels and we can have some communication," I said. "I just think your Aunt wants to watch over you and let you know that you are not alone through this ordeal."

Martha looked at me, then reached out and hugged me. I wanted so much to ask her about the young man for whom her Aunt pined. But I felt nervous. Would I be prying? Then it occurred to me that I might have a way to ask indirectly.

"Do you mind if I ask you a question about your Aunt?" I said gingerly.

"Not at all, Dear," Martha replied touching my arm as if we were old friends. "Come sit with me and have tea."

"I was wondering if your Aunt was married."

"Why, yes, she was married to a minister. We called him Papa. They were married for thirty years until his death," Martha reported, as she poured us each a cup of steaming tea.

"Oh," I said absent-mindedly. I tried to recapture the feeling I'd had. "No, that's not it." My words hung in the air.

Martha looked at me strangely. "What's not it?" she asked.

"Oh," I said suddenly realizing I had exposed my innermost thoughts. "Well, you know, you are maybe going to think I'm crazy, but I had the oddest feeling when I was making the doll—that your Aunt was pining for a young a man."

Martha's eyes grew wide and her face tightened. She put the tea- pot down on the table. "How could you know about that?" she asked clearly jarred by my statement. "Only my sister and I knew about that and we never told a soul. My Aunt died in peace knowing we had kept her secret." Martha's eyes watered.

"I'm sorry. Please don't cry. I didn't mean...I really don't know anything. It was just a feeling, that's all." I tried to comfort her. "I'm so sorry. Maybe I should go." I turned to get my things.

"No," Martha said, "don't go!" She reached over to the counter and took a tissue and blew her nose. Then she wiped her eyes. "Come, we'll sit in here." She pointed to two, stuffed chairs in her small living room. She poured a little milk and mixed a teaspoon of sugar into each cup of hot tea and handed me one. "I will tell you the story."

I felt her warmth return as I sat down. "You see," Martha began, "when my mother died my Aunt and Papa brought my sister and I to live with them. My Aunt had immigrated to this country from England and settled in a small town outside Chicago. She had met a young author, a poet, on a trip to the big city. They began to see each other, whenever she could sneak off. They were so in love..."

Martha reminisced as one who knew first-hand. "Their clandestine affair lasted about two years. My Aunt had secretly hoped to marry this young man. They lived a distance apart, so in her absence he would write poems to her. She kept each one like little treasures. Her own dreams and feelings she wrote in a diary. One day though, he went away on a trip, seeking a job. He was gone some time and when he did not return or answer her letters, my Aunt was heart-broken. She waited for him for a long time, but she never saw or heard from him, again." Martha took a sip of tea, then continued.

"It was expected for young women to marry in those days. Eventually, my Aunt felt the weight of family expectations and was obliged to accept the proposal of the local minister who wished to court her." Martha sighed. "Papa was a wonderful man."

"You see… my sister and I were just playing, one day. We were feeling a bit mischievous and bored. The weather had been too damp to go out. We dared each other to go up to the forbidden attic room. It was my sister and I who found the love letters up in the old attic trunk. Our giggling brought my Aunt up those rickety steps. We had discovered her love affair. She was so upset, she cried. She swore us to secrecy, told us if Papa found out it would kill him. So, we never told anyone…ever. It was never mentioned again."

Martha eyes were wet at the edges. My own emotions left me both teary and amazed. We hugged and Martha let tears cleanse her long held secret and her guilt of trespass.

"Your Aunt came to let me feel a tiny part of this secret…so you'd know she is with you …to let you know how much she loves you. I think she forgives you and she wants you to heal," I said. My words seemed to be forming without forethought. "I think she wants you to have faith and hope."

"Thank you," Martha said managing a little smile. She looked directly at me. "I don't know how I can ever pay you for this gift."

"You already have paid me," I said. "What you have given me in return is more valuable than money. You have helped me open a new door."

Baker's Dozen

Not long after Martha's recovery, I met a man who was in need of an artist to paint some murals for a children's arcade he was opening. I felt lucky to get the temporary job, since things at the gallery had been very slow. It was great fun painting wild animals and jungle settings on the walls of the giant indoor amusement park and I loved being a working artist again.

On my breaks, I got friendly with a few of the new hires. One woman, Sheila, and I had a few interesting conversations about creativity. I told her aside from painting, I also made dolls.

"Oh!" she said. "My mother makes dolls. She is a baker and makes little dolls for the cakes—wedding cakes and such."

"Wedding cakes and handmade dolls! That's pretty good. Does she have a shop?" I inquired.

"No, she always wanted to have one," Sheila confided, "but she just has been taking care of kids so long. She's 61 now and she's scared to start. She takes orders at home. But she really could have a shop. Her cakes, her bread and biscuits are sooo good!" Sheila moistened her lips as if in anticipation of a wonderful taste sensation.

"People know my mom's a great baker," she continued. "But, she is just afraid to take that next step, you know. I made her some business cards and we even looked at a couple of vacant places. She owns her house and she could get a loan. I think she just needs a push somehow, to believe in herself. She's a mighty strong woman. My mom raised five kids and has a dozen grands." Sheila shook her head. "Don't know what will help. She even dreams about cakes and dolls."

My wheels were turning. But I hesitated. Was this what I should be doing? I wanted more understanding of what I was tapping into, but felt it might be too intrusive. I had always disliked unsolicited help or information, but hadn't my journey started with just such a thing? What were the boundaries and how could I learn them. I had ethical questions with no answers. Should I just plunge ahead? Was all this information coming to me for a reason or was I reading into every word people said to me? Was I healing to heal, to understand this gift or was it just fascination—an artistic obsession? I certainly could not take credit for what I did. I could perhaps acknowledge myself in the creation of the art, but it was something else. It was something I had begun calling *spirit*, which or who came through me. I was simply the instrument. Should I deny what might be an important lesson?

I decided I would wait for a sign. I would allow something to lead me, although I did not know what it might be. I would wait for a dream or a fortune cookie or someone to say something that at the moment I heard it, would reverberate in my heart and soul. I did not have to wait long.

A friend called me the next day and invited me to comb through a collection of old jewelry she was planning to tag sale—remnants from her decorated picture frame hobby.

"Maybe you could find something for your dolls," she offered generously.

I loved the spring for its new leaves and flowers, but there was nothing like spring for the beginning of tag sale season in New England. I adored rising early on Saturday morning and driving through the wooded areas along the coast, past farmhouses and country stores and little villages with white-steeple churches. It was like living in a postcard. I'd lived in cities all my life, so the freedom of expansive blue sky and meadows budding with wildflowers in spring was as enchanting as the wonderful little treasures at tag sales along shady back roads.

I went cheerfully to my friend, Susan's, on Saturday, after dropping my son at soccer practice. We had coffee and she showed me around her new barn before we sat down with a bag of old jewelry she had accumulated over years of tag sales. Much of the loot was broken and pretty well picked over for her own artistic projects, but there were still worthwhile pieces from which I could create doll jewelry. As I leafed through the bits of earrings, rings, necklaces, brooches, watches and bracelets, I came across a small locket unlike any I had ever seen. It was rectangular with two intricately carved snakes entwined on the front surface and a symmetrical design along the edges giving it an aura of Native American jewelry. I instinctively opened the locket and out fell a bit of paper with some writing that was too faded to read. Chills tickled my spine. The word *recipes* popped into my head. The inside did not resemble a locket for pictures. It had depth, like a tiny pillbox, just perfect for a little message, a folded letter or some secret recipe! "This is fabulous…Can I have this?" I inquired tentatively. I was sure Susan must have overlooked it.

"Oh, yeah…isn't that a nice piece?" Susan exclaimed. "Gee, I forgot that was in there. I almost used it on the last frame I made, but it didn't really match my design.

Oh, sure. Go ahead—why don't you take it. It's perfect for a doll."

"Really? Thank you so much!" I replied to both Susan and whatever angel that stood by me. Soon, I was on my way with my locket and a small bag of assorted glass beads, bits of plated gold chains, odd silver earrings and rhinestone pieces—a bag of broken parts that I would make whole and healing, through spirit's guidance.

Over the next two weeks a doll emerged for Sheila's mom. The doll was darker than Sheila, whose complexion was a smooth, coffee with cream brown. The doll's coloring was a deep red-brown; her turquoise and earth red clothes and beads belied both African and Indian roots. The double-snaked locket at her neck contained a tiny book made up of eight ½ inch blank pages. The words *secret recipes* were written as a title on the first page. She clutched a matching cloth purse containing small coins under one arm. A three-tiered cake inside a white cake box labeled with her name and a logo—*Delilah's Delights,* filled her out-stretched hands.

I had never met Sheila's mom, the person for whom this doll was intended. While I had made a doll *of* someone I had never seen, this was the first time that I had made a doll *for* someone I had never seen. I did know why I was making the healing, as Sheila had told me of her mother's fear about being a professional baker. But beyond that I knew very little. I worried about the doll's dual cultural overtones. Where had that come from? Doubt crept into my mind.

The next day, however, I decided not to worry. Whatever lesson was in store for me as a result of my actions would come and I was intent to learn from it. I brought the doll to work with me and gave it to Sheila.

I had started to become accustomed to the "*Oh my God!*" phrase that seemed to accompany this giving act. Sheila was overwhelmed and delighted by the doll. She told me that her mother's ancestors were Native American and African American. Her mother's grandmother was Iroquois and had passed down traditional recipes to her daughter and in turn they had been passed down to Sheila's mother. In her Southern Black family, this heritage was the fabric of great stories, pride and delicious sustenance.

"Oh that little purse is so perfect! My mom is a stickler for having a purse with her at all times and always some money in the purse...like a ritual. We kids always had to have change in our pockets if we went out...a quarter at least." Sheila went on. She could not get over the cake. "And the logo! I can't believe it! I have been talking to my mom about having a logo...a label for her cake boxes. We have been discussing it for the passed week or two! How did you do this? This is so incredible...I mean I don't know how to thank you!"

"It's a gift...I'm just starting to understand it a little myself," I answered. "You don't have to thank me...you have helped me. And I hope your mom doesn't mind having helped me learn more too. I wrote her a little note of encouragement about taking first steps and following her dreams. That's what I'm doing too. We all seem to be on some kind of a journey."

I said a silent prayer of thanks when Sheila left work with her mother's doll that day. A pattern was emerging. I could hardly wait for whatever was next.

If we pay attention, life is a mosaic of intertwining patterns. Like the body itself, the universe is well-organized— an ingenious organism created by Infinite Wisdom.

The Rosary

B ut what came next was not what I anticipated. Soon after I had completed the doll for Sheila's mom, a recurring nightmare reared its ugly head. It was one I had had for as long as I could remember. As a child, I'd dream of being in a black horse-drawn carriage, riding on a bumpy dirt road near a churning gray ocean. A bitter wind would be blowing. I would be going down a hill on the way to something…I did not know what. I was cold and miserable. It was a misery beyond tears, beyond hunger, beyond thought—just bleak desolation.

I'd wake distraught, but not know what the dream was about or why it haunted me. My parents had had a print that hung above their bed when I was growing up. It was a picture of a black horse-drawn carriage against the backdrop of a gray landscape. I did not like it, but had been mesmerized by it. For a long time, I thought my dream was from that dismal picture on the wall.

Sometimes in the dream, I'd see myself in a long frock and boots that tied up the front. I'd be visiting with a woman and her daughter at their farmhouse. There was a wagon, and a barn and horses. From their kitchen window, I could see a house on the hill beyond. It was tall, dark and old. Then, suddenly I'd be at that house on the hill. It would feel strangely vacant and still. The rickety front door would swing open and creek in the wind. I'd be scared, terrified.

Sometimes I'd wake up at this point, in a cold sweat. Other times the dream scene changed and I'd be waiting on the dirt road next to the same house on the hill—waiting for someone to come down the road.

I decided about a week after the dreams started again, to stop making dolls for a while and try writing in my journal. I'd write about this child in the dream. I thought if I could write with the same intent with which I made a doll, I might be able to heal myself or at least know why I had these dreams. Little did I know, that I would find an entire life, lived by this child at some other time and place. I began to read everything I could find on reincarnation, clinical death and past life stories. When I could, I would write— allowing myself the same concentration I devoted to making a doll healing. Soon the story exploded onto the pages of my journal.

The child in my dream had been visiting a Mrs. Riley and her daughter, Anna, at their farmhouse in the Oregon territory in the mid 1800's. Her husband had been building the house on the hill for them when he died, suddenly. Anna was only a year old. So, Mrs. Riley and Anna had remained in the farmhouse. My parents met Mrs. Riley through a friend in the only nearby town. The friend knew of her financial plight, as a widow with a young child. My parents and I needed a home. We had moved from Philadelphia to my mother's chagrin, so my father could take advantage of a new business venture in the railroad. Mrs. Riley had agreed to rent the house to my parents. It meant income for her and friendship. Anna and I (the child) became inseparable, even after my baby sister was born.

When I was ten, my father's brother had come to visit us. I had never met him before and the day before his arrival, my mother and our cook (nursemaid and servant to my mother) were all abuzz with preparations for company. Anna and I were all excited since company was out of the ordinary. There was a big dinner, smoking, drinking and men talk. A day or so later my father and my uncle, who I'd come to adore, departed for a business trip. I would see my uncle again for a brief time a few days later, but by then everything would be a blur. All I would remember was his promise to return for me.

In the starting place of the dreams... *I was at Mrs. Riley's and looked out the kitchen window at my house on the hill. It was dusk. The sun had just set behind it and its dark face stared down the hill. My father was expected home that evening so, I politely refused the delicious bread pudding Mrs. Riley had just baked and started up the hill. I found the barn door open, but the horses still missing. The front door was open and creaked pitifully in the wind. A terrible chill grabbed me. I went into the house. I could smell cook's stew but could not find my mother or cook or baby sister in the kitchen or parlor. I called out to my parents, but there was only silence. I began to walk up the stairs, shaking, trembling.*

The next thing I remember is lying in the cool tall grass on the hill and Mrs. Riley and Anna hovering over me with a lantern yelling something about a shotgun and coyotes and the scent of blood. My family lay murdered and my frock was covered with their blood. Mrs. Riley scooped me up, carried me to her house and cared for me. My uncle was somehow summoned later and visited me briefly. I lived with Mrs. Riley and Anna in the shadow of my family's demise for years. I waited for my uncle's return. He had come to the funeral and rode in the caretaker's horse-drawn carriage with me to the cemetery—a long ride down a winding dirt road near the Coast.

My father had been killed in a shady business deal gone sour. He was a gambler as was my uncle. Our house had been ransacked for money and my family murdered. Mrs. Riley had been napping that afternoon due to failing health and Anna had I had been out beyond sight of the house in the high meadow with her horses.

This story and more poured out of my pen onto paper. I was flabbergasted by the detail of names and places and dates. I went to the library to check accuracy of historical facts and they seemed to match much of the writing where such things could be compared and measured. Soon, however I would have living proof.

During one of my searches of newspaper articles and books on reincarnation and past lives I came across an ad by a woman who was a hypnotherapist. Her ad referred to past lives and I had clipped it for later research. One day, out of curiosity I called her. She had an office not far from town, so I decided to make an appointment. She was a delightful, petite woman about 50 years old. She was spy and bubbly and elegant all at once. I told her about my work and inquired about hers. I hoped we would become friends as I was drawn to her and we seemed to get along instantly. Before long she requested that I make her a healing doll for her mother. She wanted to actually pay me. We decided on a barter arrangement instead. Louise would give me a reading and I would make her a doll for her 80 year-old mother who was in failing health.

I went home that day quite excited about this doll that Louise had actually asked me to create and for which she had offered to pay. But after the dinner dishes were done, I was tired. I sat down on the couch in front of the TV with my son and a box of beads and doll jewelry on my lap. I had planned to look over the bag of beads and old jewelry

I had gotten from Susan, so I rummaged through it. My mind wandered. Thoughts of Louise's mom came to me. I had a feeling of very deep blue eyes, almost violet blue and remembered having purchased an unusual pair of glass doll eyes that color a few months back. I was about to get up to search for them when I looked down at the beads in my hand. I was startled to see a rosary. I had made a rosary.

The very next morning I called Louise. "Is your mother Catholic by any chance?" I asked her. "Because I was thinking about her and I made a rosary...I haven't even started the doll yet," I said.

Louise laughed loudly. "That figures!" she yelped. "The story goes that she gave birth to me, but before she even asked to see me or hold me, she did the rosary... Hail Mary! Oh yes, that's my mother's rosary alright!" We both laughed. It was so good to laugh with someone who seemed to just accept as matter of fact what was happening to me. The day I brought the finished doll to Louise's mother, however, I could barely speak, let alone laugh. Mrs. Saxon's words echoed in my head *"You will know what you need to when the time comes."*

In a chair by the window of her living room sat a small elderly woman with a mischievous smile and twinkling violet-blue eyes. I placed the doll with her rosary next to her on the table and we both stared at it. I was seeing double. The doll was her exact portrait. She knew it, I knew it and everyone who visited her from then on, knew it. But the shock only began there. Louise's mother's married name was Mrs. Kiley. She had lived on a farm with her husband when Louise was born. They owned horses. Her husband died of a heart attack when Louise was a year old. And they took in boarders to make ends meet. When she had been able to cook in her younger years, she had been famous among her friends for her delicious bread pudding!

When I told Louise my life-long repeating dream, she said that she had awareness...some memory of having been called Anna. For a surprise birthday present some years later a friend who did not know this story gave Louise a reading from a famous past life, psychic institute. The friend had sent the institute Louise's name, age, place of birth and address. Louise received in the mail a description of herself and her life as a young pioneer in the Oregon territory.

Through the doll healing, I had been reunited with my adoptive family from another time. My parents in this life had been murdered in the past life; my father's attraction to speculation and gambling permeated both. The funeral painting above their bed had been a gift to my parents — a soul memory of the consequences my father's gambling addiction.

Louise, my friend again, named my work *Dolls For The Soul*.

Grandma's Hands

Louise's office was just at the outskirts of town in a beautiful old house that had been converted to office spaces. There was a room available on the ground floor that had not been renovated and still held its "turn of the century" look. It had originally been a kitchen and while there were no appliances there was a porcelain kitchen sink and some old glass-faced cupboards along one wall. Large windows on either side of the cupboard boasted their original panes of glass and let in plenty of afternoon light. A door at one corner of the room, led outside to a yard where five tall pines stood majestically in a sacred circle on the back lawn. It was perfect for a studio of my own!

Louise gave me the security deposit for it and within a few weeks I had moved in with my supplies. I decorated the place for the season with lace curtains, shelves filled with dolls I'd made, angels ornaments and small white Christmas lights. I got a coffee maker, tea pot, cups, and a cookie jar. I added hanging green ferns and a vase with fresh flowers. The perfume of vanilla candles, sage and eucalyptus created an inviting ambiance. A month later the local paper came to interview me for a feature article for the arts section. Soon people were knocking on the door asking me to make a *Healing Doll* for them, or a loved one. Each one brought a lesson for me, for which I was very grateful.

One day a woman came to the studio. She seemed a bit timid at first. I offered her a comfortable chair across from my table and a cup of tea. I had come to realize that although people came to talk about their problems, their healing usually did not have anything to do with their own evaluations of their situation. So, I let each talk as they needed to and offered a sympathetic ear. I offered only a *Healing Doll* as a solution. On this particular day, Enid Pearl said that she had seen the article in the local paper. "It was so interesting, I had to come meet you."

Enid Pearl said she had been feeling down lately and didn't know why. She said her chronic pain had worsened slightly since the weather had turned cold again, but mostly she was feeling sad. She talked a little about her mixed heritage and about her children, now grown with their own families. She stayed for about an hour talking, looking around at the dolls on the shelf and drinking tea I'd made for us. When she left I had an order for her doll and healing.

About three weeks later I put in a call to Enid. Her doll had taken shape—but an unusual shape. I felt I needed to speak with her before I could be comfortable in giving the doll to her. Her doll was a woman about Enid's age (at least 65 years old, I estimated.) The doll had one hand that was smooth and youthful and one that looked arthritic. She was dressed in a white eyelet and forest green cotton with white embroidered lace. Her auburn hair was swept up softly in a bun. But what was bizarre is that her body construction was that of a woman, seven-months pregnant!

Enid picked up the phone. "Hi Enid, how are you? I wanted to let you know your doll will be ready next week, but I needed to ask a question. I wanted to know if you had had any difficult pregnancies. You mentioned you had grown children?" I asked.

"Why, yes...two children," she said. "And yes I was very ill... how did you know that?"

"I didn't, but your doll seems to be an older woman who does and there is something coming through about a pregnancy and healing." I said.

"Oh, my!" Enid exclaimed. "Thank you...well I'll have to come down and see the doll" she said.

I expected Enid would do just that, but several weeks went by before she did come in again. She came by one afternoon and again seemed very hesitant. But when she saw the doll she cried. "That is my grandmother," she finally said turning toward me. "She practically raised us herself. I took a long time to come here again because I was afraid it might be her. But she is just beautiful and just as I remember her. She used to sew all our dresses in eyelet fabric and she was a great seamstress. Everyone came to her in the neighborhood for her wonderful embroidery until she got the arthritis She had rheumatoid arthritis and her hands became damaged..." Enid said as she rubbed a finger over the doll's one gnarled hand.

"And the pregnancy?" I asked.

A tear flowed down one of her cheeks. Enid took a tissue from her purse and wiped it away. "I was seven months pregnant with my first child when my grandmother took ill with pneumonia...I was bed ridden during my pregnancy and the doctor told me I'd lose the baby if I made the trip to see her. I was heartbroken. My grandmother kept calling for me to come. She died before the birth of my child and I never got to say goodbye or go to the funeral. I never forgave myself and I have always felt like she never forgave me, either." Enid did not bother to wipe her tears, again. I put my arm around her shoulder.

"I think she has come through to let you know it is time to forgive yourself. There is a lot of love for you and understanding. How old was your grandmother when she passed?"

"She was 63 years old," Enid said. Then she looked at me as if seeing me for the first time…"That's funny, I just turned 63," she said.

"They say 'God works in mysterious ways' you know. I think you wandered in here for a reason, even if you did not know what would come of it."

"This is so amazing," Enid said. "I have been carrying around this grief for so long, I didn't even realize how it was affecting me." Enid looked at the vase of fresh flowers on the shelf next to her doll. "Light pink roses were her favorite!" she said.

The Silent Writer

Not long after Enid 's visit another woman came into the studio. She walked with a cane and coughed from the moment she stepped in out of the cold. Joanne could barely speak, but was finally able to tell me that she had cerebral palsy. It took her two hours of excruciating labored breathing and vocalizing to tell me that she remembered the fever that had wracked her four year-old body and brought her to the edge of death. She remembered the loss of sight and sound and movement and speech. And she remembered regaining some of her life back…but never all.

She felt frustrated and angry at the way people treated her because of her disability and she wanted to scream, but could not. Her brother had recently given her a computer for her birthday, but it sat unused because she was afraid to try. Her hands could not accommodate a typist's movement and speed. She thought I could help her. She wanted to write a novel, a love story. I offered her a *Healing Doll* with the explanation that I did not know what was to come, but that whatever healing I would make for her would be done with the most sincere truth of spirit, not my will.

When she left that day I was emotionally drained. I went home to rest and reflect on the enormity of the undertaking…the sheer responsibility of having people have enough faith in my work to help them. I prayed and asked for guidance in this new level of healing. Joanne would get a healing doll that would be different from any I'd made before.

Her doll would be a speaking doll. Its joyful face emerged from the clay, mouth opened and talking to me. The fact that I heard voices or communicated with spirits was no longer a problem for me. The voices belonged to spirits that were obviously related to me or to the people who sought me out. They spoke only of healing the heart and were filled with love. (Of course, I would not go into a doctor's office and say as much, knowing that "hearing voices "might not be viewed like the flu.) But my work was a conscious healing and as such I had come to trust the process. Although the term *speaker doll* came through to me, the concept of a speaker doll came from a Native American tradition, as I would later find out. My work as a modern healer was just beginning to evolve, but in traditions that were many thousands of years old!

When Joanne came to get her finished doll she was delighted. Although the doll was not a family member, she recognized the face as a guide and the essence of the work as a helper. She was overjoyed with her doll and could not wait to take her home. I would not know for several months just what effect the healing would have.

It was the following spring when I ran into Joanne and she told me she had joined a writing group and had begun her novel. She asked me if I would read it and give her some feedback. I told her it was a very good start, as I was delighted she had taken the risk to begin living her dream. I told her to use her doll …to put it by the computer and meditate before she began to write. "A good author writes from their life experience," I said —repeating what a wise woman once told me. Don't be afraid…I think you have a lot to say. It was the first time I had advised someone to use their doll as a tool in their healing process. It sounded like something from a sci-fi movie, but it felt right.

Several months later, I attended the writing group. Joanne was still working on her romance novel, but had also brought her most recent work and asked me to read it aloud to the group for her. I agreed to do so. The piece was a beautifully crafted poem about a four-year old child plunged into darkness, silence and pain by an illness she could not fathom. It was the memory of a five year old regaining the use of her eyes, her ears, her limbs, but not her voice. It was the words of a child whose first utterance came later, in the form of a scream.

A Man on a Mission

One evening, a few weeks before Christmas a man and woman came into the studio. It was getting dark and I had been preparing to leave. My dog had been with me that day and was already in the car looking forward to the ride home and dinner. I had checked in with my son and told him I'd be home shortly. I had put away my materials and turned off the coffee maker.

"Oh," the man said…"we just heard about you from Louise and thought we could order some dolls. Are you still open?" The word "some" was not something I had ever heard before. "Uh, sure…I have a little time before closing. Come in, please."

"Some dolls" turned out to be four. Although nervous about doing so many at once, I was thrilled at my good fortune. But what was even more thrilling was what happened next. As the man—Daniel, began to talk to me I saw a doll emerging. Daniel was Caucasian, but the doll in my vision was Black and African…from South Africa. The doll wore traditional garments. His essence was balanced in the feminine and masculine principle and he held the role of teacher to this man, Daniel, sitting in front of me. I was so astonished to be seeing a vision and to be talking to a real person at the same time that I felt that I could barely keep my attention on Daniel's words. When Daniel finished speaking about himself I asked him what he did for a living.

"Do you travel?" I asked.

"Yes," he said, "I travel extensively for work."

"Out of the country?" I inquired.

"Yes, as a matter of fact, quite a bit." He seemed pleasantly surprised that I was leading him toward something about himself that he hadn't revealed. I didn't know anything more than what my vision imparted.

"To Africa?" I continued.

"The Middle East," he said.

"Actually, I think you might be going to South Africa. There seems to be someone there for you to meet. If you don't mind your doll will be some representation of this energy that this person needs to bring you."

Daniel said he'd be open to whatever I made for him. His wife's turn was next and she also spoke of things that were very different than what her healing would impart. Her Dutch Aunt would come through with some very important healing to help her as well.

I was very excited by the encounter. Just as my healing journey seemed predictable and complete, a sudden turn in the road would push me through yet another door, to a deeper reality. I drove home in a hurry to get dinner on the table and to rest up for the preparation of some dolls. Within the month Daniel's African doll was made and his company had informed him that he would be traveling to South Africa come February.

Autumn

Angel

Doctor

Twin Spirit

Wizard

Cat Goddess

Healer

Grandmother

Bubbie

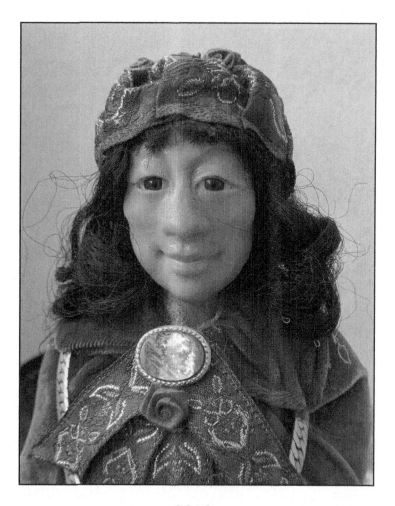

Meisha

Bless the Children

Just around Valentine's Day another surprise awaited me. I had never made a healing doll for children, but during the last few weeks in February I was to have not only one chance, but two.

Marie came first. She had also seen the paper and came to me *as a last resort*. She had taken her niece, who was living with her, to a doctor, a minister and a therapist, but nothing helped the thirteen year-old teen. She explained that the girl could not sleep and had terrible anxiety. She would be up most of the night and could only sleep curled up on the couch with her head in her aunt's lap, with the light and TV both on. Even then, she suffered from nightmares and sudden waking. The child had been the victim of abuse in her very young years and the aunt felt I should know this. I explained that I would do my best to ask for a healing to help her.

When she left I began the child's doll. The next day, while I was working on the aunt's order another woman came into the studio. "I've come to see if you can help my daughter. She is ten years old. Do make doll healings for children?" she inquired.

"Uh…yes," I said hesitantly. "I have begun to do doll healing for children. Please sit down and we can talk a little."

Donna sat down and we had tea. She poured out her heart. She told me her daughter had a rare eye disease and that it created such terrible problems for her in school.

"The problem is that she cannot distinguish the lettering from the page," Donna explained. "The black becomes white and as the letters are fading the eye tries to keep up with the movement and the letters appear to be falling off the end of the page. No one believed her for a few years and she suffered great ridicule. Now that we have found out that it is a real disease, the only solution is colored glasses. But the color has to change every two or three weeks. She is still teased all the time. She comes home so emotionally drained and depressed. The problem is though, that she hates dolls, so I don't know if this is the right thing to do or not…"

I listened. I had known many children in my life that had faced terrible ridicule because of their disabilities. I was very sure that it was no accident that Donna had come to me. "I will make something for her." I reassured this distraught mother. "Don't worry, I will call you in a few weeks."

I was alone in the studio the rest of the day. I prayed for guidance and listened intently. I let the images flow through my hands to the clay and soon a child's face emerged with a bright smile and sparkling brown eyes that had the gift of real sight. The child had psychic intuition. She was an *old soul*. "There you are," I said aloud to the little clay face. I dressed her in purple and gave her plenty of pockets and a pouch, filled with shells and crystals and ceramic turtles, fish, and frogs.

When Donna came back several weeks later she too cried tears, but of joy. "This looks just like my daughter …when she was well." She took a picture of her daughter from her wallet. A child of six peered out with clear eyes and a happy smile.

The next day, I completed the healing for Marie's

niece. The doll was a young woman of royalty with great compassion and power. Her eyes were kind and loving. She exuded self-esteem, protection and confidence. Marie thought she was beautiful and could not wait to take her home to her niece. She whisked the doll away like a mother rushing home with precious medicine for a sick child.

It was some time later before I heard from Donna and Marie. Donna came back to the studio a few weeks after picking up her doll. She wanted to thank me and tell me what had transpired. She said her daughter, upon hearing she was receiving a doll was not pleased at all. But, when she saw the doll, the child grabbed it and ran into her room. Donna said that her daughter was in her room quite a long time. When she emerged, Donna noticed that her child had cleared off her dresser and set all her most precious items in a circle around the doll.

Donna related that now when her daughter comes home from school she goes into the room—sometimes for half an hour—and soon she is in a much better mood. "I saw a transformation taking place. But I had to tell you what she said yesterday. She came out of her room and told me that she had seen all the people who had ever loved her in that doll…even the doll-maker!"

Chills danced up my spine and a lump was in my throat. I could not thank Donna enough for coming to tell me what had happened. I knew this child was very special.

A few days later a letter arrived in the mail from Marie. She said that her niece had loved the doll and had placed it next to her bed. For the first night in a long time, the child had actually slept through the night in her own bed. "You and I know that this is about FAITH…thank you for the work you are doing, my dear." she wrote. "I am so glad I took the chance to come to see you. Thank you so much for what you have done for us."

The Door of Time

One day, as spring was blooming again and fragrant flowers filled the air, a friend of mine asked me to make a doll healing for her middle-aged sister who was recovering from a breakdown. She was having a birthday and celebrating a major milestone in her new integration of mind and spirit. I went to see Charlotte, a woman for whom I had made a doll healing a month before.

I would ask Charlotte to make me some special herbal incense for this doll healing. I felt that smell was of major importance in the healing and needed the expertise of a healer who worked with aromatic therapy and herbs. I would cleanse the doll in these and add them in the pockets of the clothing.

Charlotte had a gift for knowing herbs and making her own healing incense. But it was not until she received her *Healing Doll* that she knew more about her connection to this wonderful gift. I had felt the redheaded woman doll emerge for her as a mother...someone with whom she really needed to connect. There seemed to be a very big hole in Charlotte's heart where mother love should have resided. Charlotte had lost her mother as a young child and it seemed that this transcended not only this lifetime but the past as well. The doll that emerged was a mother figure from another time; a woman that lived in Europe in the sixteenth century. This woman raised geese and tended a vegetable and herb garden. Upon receiving her *Healing*

Doll, Charlotte told me that red hair was a family trait, even though her hair was dyed blonde.

But Charlotte would have a deeper vision in the first few weeks of having her *Healing Doll*. Charlotte told me that she had sat with her doll in the living room one day. Before long, she began having a vision that felt almost like a trance. "It unfolded like a dream," she said. In her vision, she saw herself as a child picking healing herbs, roots and bark with her mother…walking through woods and fields as her mother explained the healing properties and how to use the various things they collected in their basket.

Then the scene shifted. Charlotte was now alone in the meadow picking flowers and greens that her mother had sent her to find, when she came across several soldiers. One soldier was very seriously injured and his comrades were deciding what to do with him. The child offered to help. She knew how to make a poultice, how to dress his wound and what he needed to survive. She knew he would die if he did not get some treatment.

The soldiers were very angry with her and told her that she could be killed for trying to make medicine. But they decided at last to let her save the life of the young man. When Charlotte finished her treatment, she went directly home to tell her mother what had happened. Upon hearing the story her mother quickly gathered up the child's belongings and a basket of food. Then her mother took her to the far end of the forest where a small stream ran down the hill into the valley and beyond. She told Charlotte that she must never tell anyone about healing the soldier or what she knew about herbs and healing. Most importantly, Charlotte must never return. The child was to follow the stream to the river and then beyond to the city. The mother explained to the child that as long as she followed her instructions; their lives would be saved. The child and mother cried as they parted forever.

It was only in this vision that Charlotte realized that her mother would be found by the soldiers and killed for being a witch. Women healers by the thousands were being exterminated by the Inquisition, branded as witches.

Charlotte's vision paralleled actual events in history. At least a million (many estimates are higher) women healers were executed in Europe during the time of the Inquisition. Healing and mid-wifery were the domain of women in Europe (as well as in other parts of the world) for centuries, before medicine came under control of men, the Church and government rulers. Charlotte's doll had brought her an understanding of the depth of her sorrow and a connection to the mother for whom she longed.

Many Thanks to Jim

Several months passed and by the late spring I was beginning to feel drained. I was preparing for my first show
and had little time for much else. I decided a tag sale would
be a good way to do my spring-cleaning and make a little
extra money at the same time. It was during this spring rite
that I was to meet someone that would renew my spirit.

As my ability to know more about the nature of each
healing increased (more in-depth information came to
me), the more my need for a response from the people
whose lives I touched, grew. I wanted to know concretely
that my work was making a difference. I had no idea that
the weekend was to bring just what I needed.

I set out my items for the tag sale in my driveway on a
sunny Saturday morning. The sale went very well; neighbors and passers-by rummaged through an impressive
amount of pots and pans, gift boxes, children's toys, books,
old records, tools, lawn furniture, frames and assorted
household appliances—all of which I had accumulated,
but none of which I had used in some time. By mid-day
I decided to empty a closet in the dining room where I
kept some additional items—an old lamp, some games
and sports equipment my son had outgrown among other
things. They were stuffed in boxes behind the shelves lined
with dolls I was making. I set the dolls on the porch temporarily, as I pulled stuff out of the closet and replenished
my driveway sale.

Before I could put the dolls back in the closet, a few people had gathered at the sale tables. I decided to leave the dolls where they were…perhaps I might get an inquiry, I thought. At any rate they were in the shade and up higher than the dog could reach. I turned my attention to a woman holding up a set of potholders for a price check. Just then, a man came riding up to the driveway on his bicycle. He stopped in mid-cycle and perused the tables of wares. Then he glanced at the porch. "What's up there?" he asked. "Can I see those?" He pointed to the dolls.

"Why, yes…those are dolls that I make." He seemed even more interested. He got off his bike and set the kickstand. I thought it unusual that a man of about 40 or so would be interested in dolls, unless he had heard about the work I did. He said that he had not. He lived in another state and was here visiting family. He told me his name was Jim and he was a writer who appreciated art. I thanked him for the compliment.

Jim was particularly attracted to a wizard doll I had just completed. I had made it for a teacher who had come into my shop a few months earlier requesting a wizard for a display in his astronomy class. He had neither paid me nor returned to claim it, so for now I had decided to hold onto it. Jim, the cyclist wished to have it. I told him I would make one for him or I could make him a *Healing Doll*. He looked at me strangely. I explained what it was that I did, as best as I could. After a few moments he said that it sounded so unusual that he had to have a *Healing Doll*. "But, I hope it turns out to be a wizard!" he laughed giving me a deposit and his mailing address. Then, he walked back to his bike and rode off.

I was really happy about having left the dolls out that day. I proceeded to make Jim's doll. Within a month, a doll that was a representation of this mother came through. I knew he would not be happy. He seemed to have a stressful connection to this woman who was conservative and religious. But, I knew it was a very important lesson and one that he needed to address soon. I sensed that her health was deteriorating, and I felt her vacillating between this world and the next.

The lesson was about his reaction to people with more conservative views than his, so it was important for him to come to terms with his reactions to his mother. She was his teacher. In doing the work of reconciliation, his ability to speak out—when confronted with views that were more conservative than his own—would later be enhanced. I told him that someday he would be an important voice writing about world events. He needed to be objective. His mother was a gift. He needed to see her in a different light. I hoped he would be able to see that through this healing.

I sent the doll off to him wrapped in the usual bubble wrap and prayed that he did not hate it, because of all things not a wizard, it would be least what he wanted. I had experienced that the person who got the healing was often surprised by what they received, but most often they were receptive. I was not sure about Jim, though—not until a month later, when I received his letter.

Dear Nina Ayin,

"Do you need another testimonial? I suspect need is not the issue. Connection is, connection is where the value lies.

I was giddy with embarrassment after I decided to get a doll from you. Telling my wife I had ordered a doll from a psychic doll-maker. My doubts and skepticism. Several friends I told, embarrassed. I waited and prepared myself for the possibility of not liking what I received. I was fairly confident it would be beautiful. So it came, a notice that the package arrived. I took a good friend with me to pick it up. I was eager, anxious and still embarrassed. I had not told him about the doll yet. He is an artist, an iconoclast, with his own dim view of worldly things. We drove to the post office and picked up the package, then to the tool rental place. I needed to pick up a jack hammer, that most manly of tools. I had never used one before but needed it for a project.

While the woman was drawing up the paper work, I brought my friend to the car to open the package from you. I wanted a witness. And I liked the juxtaposition of being in this bend-this-break-that-cut-this rental place and opening my psychic doll package.

I read your letter first. We peeked through the bubble wrap. Was I disappointed? Yeah. And amused by my unrelenting, romantic foolishness in spite of what I know of the world. I wanted a wizard. You made me a mother.

You were right. My mother had very much been preoccupying my thoughts when I met you. I had been visiting with her under stressful conditions. You were right in describing her as a proper, controlling, narrow-minded, critical and religious person with whom I've had difficulty. My father passed when I was ten, the oldest of four children. My mother divided her time between kids and working in the church rectory on affairs of the church, the priest and nuns.

Recently, a family crisis for a sibling triggered some old painful wounds. Before the doll arrived and still, I have been grappling with an anger toward my mother unlike I had ever known- at a time when she is growing more feeble, her health steadily in retreat. She recently had a fall and has surrendered to her pain.

I see her needs. I am not a patient caregiver and my anger only heightens my aversion to spending time with her, which exacerbates the eldest son's guilt for the plight of his widowed mother.

The doll represents a woman self-assured, elegant, strong and whole. It stands on my dresser next to my bed. I see it and think of those latent attributes in my mother and it is a great reminder of what could be, or could have been. Through a kind of meditation on the doll woman I've begun to recall some of the many positive things my mother provided and assisted me with, that she tries to pass on to her grandchildren.

Last week I envisioned taking her for a walk through a nice park near her house, a park she never visits. It seemed a simple pleasant, notion—-helping her each beyond her physical limits, outside the confines of her house, while enabling me a physical outlet through which I can share my vitality. When I went to her house to do this she refused. She cried, rare tender connection.

I hold onto the vision of walking with her, the vision of her enjoying it, of her getting stronger and marveling at the beauty around her. I've also decided to spend some time photographing her in her house. I'm not sure where this will lead or where the notion came from. Or maybe I do.

I still wonder about the doll, how it will fit, where it might lead over time. The joy and hope in its eyes, the tenderness in its fine hands. When I first noticed the doll's flowers, they struck me as lilies-of-the-valley, the flower my mother speaks of as her favorite. I saw and cried.

Thank you, for your healing gift"...Jim

I had come to learn an important lesson. The healing that came forth was always the one needed as I was not the one giving it ...it came through me. I could not know all these things by myself. I could do this work if not guided by the universe or spirit. I could not provide such specific details from almost no information, if it were not for Divine Love's direction. And while the person who got the healing was often surprised by what they received, most often they were receptive. In some cases, it transformed their lives...and in doing so, transformed my own.

Teachers Abound

As time went on, I found that the healings produced changes in people's lives in more and more profound ways, just like the contact with my doll had produced for me. My life had been completely transformed by my unusual encounter with Mrs. Saxon and now my *Intuitive Healing Dolls* seemed to be bringing other wonderful results, as well.

A woman who had come to one of my first workshops where I spoke about my work asked me to make her a *Healing Doll*. She was a doll-maker also. Later she would become a friend, as well. What came through for this woman, was an Egyptian doll who was a scholar, a priest, and a mathematician. The doll came in as a helper, someone to remind her of who she really was and the information she had used from another time.

But the story is better told in the recipient's own words:

"It was right before Valentine's Day in 1999 when I received my first doll from Nina. I had eagerly awaited her or his arrival in my life, but had no idea what the doll would look like. I knew that it would be special and unlike other doll I had ever owned.

See, I like dolls. I've always liked dolls. As an only child growing up, my stuffed animals or dolls were my only companions on the trips I would take—my imaginary journeys to the Old West, Africa, Timbuktu, on a plane or under the sea. When

I was little, each Christmas I hoped for a new doll to add to my store of ratty haired, white, blue eyed, plastic dolls. In fact, I was into dolls so strongly that when I was 12 my mother gave me a two foot tall, freckled faced, eyeglass-wearing, blonde-haired, talking doll, instead of the microscope that I kept hinting at after talking about that doll.

That was the last doll my mother gave me, but here and there varying friends had gifted me with a doll. Now, I was to receive this new doll while I was in a transition period between jobs and living off of unemployment. I needed something to lift my mood and to bring something stimulating into my life.

Nina came to visit me. After the usual pleasantries, she carefully unpacked a large object from the suitcase she had brought with her. Slowly she unwrapped my doll and then she stood it before me. I was speechless as I looked at the doll's black hair, brown eyes, brown skin, beautiful blue robes, brass breastplate encrusted with varying gemstones, welcoming smile and hands full of more gifts. Here in miniature stood the image of a woman who I considered to be like my sister—another only child who I had found connection with through my spiritual tradition.

I was overjoyed. The doll brought close to me someone who lived over 3000 miles away and now I had her here with me everyday. Immediately, I named her My Sister. But there was even more for me to learn that evening. There was all this information that Nina had received as she was creating My Sister.

This information was given to me on a sheet of paper and spoke of the doll's history and her purpose for coming into my life. I read through the message and found only one part bit mystifying. There was this information about me and geometry that made no sense to me.

In school, algebra and geometry were my least favorite subjects. Now, I was being told that geometry would play an important role in my future life. That made absolutely no sense to me. Up until this point in my life I had proved to my mother and my teachers of the past that I had no use for learning all of those geometry corollaries, axioms and formulas. My "good manners" kept me from complaining or voicing any negativity to Nina about this out of sync piece of information. I thanked Nina for the doll and began living with My Sister doll everyday.

After a couple of weeks, a friend of mine told me about a job opening for an office manager where she worked and asked for my resume. Within the next two days I was being interviewed and then hired for the job. Imagine my surprise when I found out that geometry was used everyday in my new workplace, an engineering and architecture firm. Just a few months later, I found myself using that high school geometry when I performed some junior engineering for one of the staff engineers.

My Sister doll's prediction had come true. The geometry that I had scorned as a teenager I had finally used in a work situation. My old geometry knowledge had a reason for being in my head. This was something I would never have foreseen. Now, I was left to ponder the other information contained in the message that Nina had given me about my doll."

—*Uzuri*

⤸

Another woman after attending a workshop to learn the art that I had begun teaching, made a doll that enabled her to write about an ill relative. She was so moved by the experience that she decided to become a doll-maker herself and in doing so found a path to her retirement at age 60.

It was not uncommon for a person to receive a doll portrait from me of someone he or she had not seen or heard from in many years. For one writer, her doll represented a girl who had been a singer during their high school years and who had created a lasting impression. Did the healing influence the author? Who's to say...but her new spiritually uplifting songs still inspire all who hear them.

Both men and women living with cancer and other life-threatening illnesses have told me that the healing dolls they received from me continue to give them the courage and strength to face the doctors and hospital visits for check-ups, as they remain in remission. Their survival and well-being are in part due to self–care—love, connection to spirituality and positive thoughts do play a role in a good prognosis. Some people believe that love and prayer can create healing miracles.

The power of the spiritual connection we have to each other has come to my attention not only upon completion of a healing, but actually during the time I am preparing the healing. One time, I was making a doll for a woman in her late forties and an elderly, kind, little female doll came through. I had been recently given a gift of some exquisite white lama hair entwined with silvery threads. When I gave the elderly doll some of this hair, I immediately heard the words *"fairy god-mother"* and saw the color pink as the choice for the outfit. Actually, it was a shocking pink and I was very unsure that it was right, initially. I asked for guidance and again I was directed to hot pink. Having learned to trust the spiritual process that guided me, I dressed the little doll as directed. I sent the doll and the reading off to its owner. I waited hoping that the color and the meaning were clear and precisely what was needed. This reply came soon after:

Dear Nina,

I just received my doll and I'm so thrilled. She arrived on a perfect day for her to enter my life. It's a day of things I'm displeased with about myself as a well as a day of changing responses on my part for the future. It's like I'm on the cusp and ready to fly in a direction where I have full trust of myself, while at the same time trying to shake loose from the self recriminations that make me doubt myself.

…When I first saw her, I was looking to see who she resembled. She didn't resemble anyone in particular from my life, not anyone. All I kept thinking is that she looks like me, though not really like me, but like I would like to look when I achieve her wisdom. Then the words "fairy God-mother" popped into my head., but I felt silly acknowledging them, until I read your letter…you wrote how you intuited that she was like a "fairy God-mother" figure to me. That feels so perfect, so hopeful, so adoring, so alluring. I feel that if I let her in, I could feel light again, happy, joyful, carefree, unburdened by the heavy weight of responsibility that I wear constantly. And she is carrying the objects (birds and seashells) that I adore, that make me feel light and youthful. I love watching birds and talking to them in my own way—and seashells make me think of how much I love walking on the beach and feeling the oneness of the lapping waves that seem to align my internal rhythm to the rhythm of the water, the sand and the air. Those are the two absolute close to my heart loves. I don't know how you knew that but you did!

…The color pink and the feminine objects she is wearing is another delightful surprise. You are right about my issues concerning appearances and femininity. I've tended toward dark colors that I can hide behind. But recently I've been wearing a lot of red and pink and I've been buying delicate heart shapes

and sweet pearls in necklace and earrings, a divergent path form my usual more imposing taste. And at work, I've been sending around my memos on pink paper, which is totally new for me. So maybe with these first steps, my fairy God-mother can help me let my fuller inner femininity emerge, and allow that buried part of me to break through the powerful/providing/pillar of strength image that has become too overbearing for my light-hearted self to breathe the air—and take its rightful exalted place.

Looking into her eyes, all my anxiousness of the past couple of days is melting from the warmth of her understanding and loving smile...she is clearly telling me that I need to respond to myself with love, and I'm warmed by how good that feels. If I can feel love for myself, I can share my love with those around me. It feels so simple, so right, especially compared to the anger I've been carrying around lately. I see now the hurt I'm causing myself and others by responding in anger. The anger dissipates so easily when love is let in. I feel accepted, when I look at my wise fairy God-mother doll...it makes me want to weep with joy. Thank you, thank you a zillion times.

In true joy, JNK

෴

Not long after that I made another doll. This one needed butterfly fabric, which I dressed it in without question. I had never met the recipient and knew nothing about her, except her name, age and a mailing address, as was often the case. The doll healing had been ordered as a gift for her by a relative.

However, upon receiving her gift, the woman wrote me to say she had felt something unusual happening a few weeks before she received the doll. Her mood had been improving; her anxiety had been lessening. She had begun to feel hope returning. She said that she had decided to attend a butterfly exhibit at a major museum in the city near her home. She and some friends sat in a huge enclosed exhibit room at the museum surrounded by thousands of live butterflies from all over the world. It was a transformational experience. When she received the doll dressed in butterflies it was like a thunderbolt...a sign of confirmation for her that Divine healing was taking place.

I had come to learn that the process involved not only the portrait, but every aspect of the art—clothing, hair, jewelry. Everything had a meaning. Often the reading and visions would come to me only after these details were attended to...nothing could be overlooked.

I will never forget the struggle I had one time with what appeared to be myself. Luckily the employees at the fabric store knew me, as I walked around arguing with what seemed to be an imaginary person. I was talking aloud in the store to an invisible someone that only I could hear. "I don't like that fabric...that can't be right ..." I said.

Finally, I gave up and left without the black and white fabric I was being directed toward by Spirit. But that night I couldn't sleep. I'd wake up knowing I had to go back to the store to buy that fabric I did not like, for a woman who had wanted a doll for her mother. Things had been a little difficult from the start. The daughter had insisted she send me a picture of her mother. Even when I informed her that I did not work from pictures, that I was not making a portrait *of* her mother, but *for* her mother — she still said she must send it. I finally gave in, telling her that she could send a photo in a tightly sealed envelope. I did not know at the time why she insisted on this, but as I had no intention of looking at the photo, I agreed.

The next day, realizing that I had been resisting this healing, I went and bought the black and white material. I created the outfit, and when the work was complete it turned out to be a very thorough healing. I felt the person receiving the work would be greatly soothed and comforted. I was pleased with every aspect as well, except for the eye color. I was not sure I had gotten the color just right. For this healing it needed to match closely to the recipient. It was then that I remembered the photo the daughter had sent.

I went to my desk and rummaged through some unopened mail. I found the envelope containing the photo. I opened it. Laughter accompanied my surprise. In the photo, stood a woman dressed in the exact outfit with the black and white patterned fabric that I had just created for her doll! I heard the spirits roar with laughter, too.

Our will resists, because we do not recognize the teachers that cross our path each day. We argue and dig in our heels, not recognizing our soul's wisdom, our destiny. Our lessons continue, however. Teachers come ad infinitum, offered by the grace of Unconditional Love.

The View From Above

O ne day, I invited one of my first workshop student's, Frankie, to my house for dinner. Over dessert, we got to talking about dreams. I confided in him that I had had a disturbing dream a few days before. In the dream, I was fatally injured and was near death before I awoke. I remembered the sensation of losing blood and that I was dying from a wound inflicted by someone I did not recognize. The dream felt so real, as some dreams do, and its aftermath had left me perplexed.

He told me that he had a meditation that would enable me to go into the dream scenario in an awake state and not only retrieve the dream sequence, but obtain more information. I had often tried to fall back asleep when I had been woken suddenly in the middle of a "good" dream , but had never been able to do it too successfully. Someone had told me to lie with my head in the same position it had been just upon waking, but that was hard to remember. So I was skeptical about the meditation, as well, but decided to try it anyway.

I cleared the dining room dishes and sat in a comfortable chair in the living room. I closed my eyes, breathed and listened as Frankie guided me with his voice. I relaxed. Soon I was able to visualize the dream , I was back in the room prior to the injury being inflicted. With my friend's guidance I was able to move within the dream and open the space around me, peer into rooms and see doors, windows and furniture. I was able to walk around, touch objects, see colors and sense things, like the time of day. I then walked outside, finding out information I needed to know like names, places and dates.

When I was satisfied with what I had gained, we ended the meditation. I was exhilarated. It was like flying in a dream state only with control over one's own actions and movements. It was not unlike hypnosis, but I was aware I could do this by myself. I could teach myself to make a 360 degree turn in this meditative state and I could go backward and forward in time!

I had always had a hard time wrapping my mind around the *"all time is happening at the same time"* concept about which I had heard. Now my consciousness shifted. Something clicked. I had just sat in my living room in present time, inside a dream from past time about a possible event in future time. If one considered dreams to qualify as a substantial reality, then I had presently gone back to a possible future.

Although some part of me was still skeptical, it was not such a stretch for me to validate my dreams; some of them had actually transpired. My dreams had at times been a reliable premonition tool, a mirror of my emotions or a door through which I had received guidance. Others who had had dreams with messages for me in the past, had been accurate as well. Placing myself in a meditative state had enhanced my *intuitive imagery*, the name I gave to my process. The bits of information that came to me during the healing work, did so while I was in creative meditation. Now, I had the next step...and I thanked Frankie for being my teacher, as well as my student.

I could not wait to try my new skill during a doll healing. I thought I could verify the experience if I could repeat it during a doll healing. I did not have to try hard. During my next doll healing, I went into a relaxed state as I sculpted. Suddenly, I found myself standing on the landing at the top of a long flight of stairs. I looked down into the foyer below. I was in the home that had belonged to the grandmother of the woman for whom I was making the doll. I knew this intuitively.

All at once, the front door in the foyer came whipping open and in bolted a little girl of about ten. She was laughing and out of breath from playing. She was a bit disheveled, her dress and hair as one might expect from a child who's been playing outdoors. Soon her grandmother was standing next to her, scolding in a gentle yet firm manner. I could tell by the conversation that she loved this child, but the girl was a little too high-spirited for the grandmother's taste. Taking the child in hand, they walked away from the foyer, down a hall to the left of where I stood.

From that brief interlude I was able to ascertain the nature of the relationship and the time period which was the early 1940's. The grandmother felt it her responsibility to teach the child proper manners and dress. The grandmother was a respected church lady, and the matriarch of her family. She wanted the girl, all sweaty and dirty from rough play to behave in a manner more befitting the young women she was soon to become—and to stay out of harm's way. She felt protective of this child. Trouble had no trouble finding Black children in particular, in this time and place. So, the grandmother kept a watchful eye.

After the grandmother and granddaughter left the foyer, I consciously walked down the stairs and stood where they had been standing moments before. I could smell the fresh scent of bleach that emanated from the white curtains adorning the windows. I ran my hands over the oiled, dark wood that trimmed the foyer. I peered into the adjacent parlor and down the hall along the stairs that led to the kitchen, where I could intuit they had gone for a cool drink.

Here I was in the present and the past at the same time. The future would hold the verification of my experience. The doll healing was for a woman now in her 60's who would recognize her grandmother from the portrait and information I had gathered during a moment of their time together 50 years ago. Without Spirit's guidance I could have not *known* nor made the wonderful grandmother doll.

The grandmother doll came dressed in traditional clothes, hairstyle, and adornments of African decent. She had relinquished her proper church apparel—her clothes *and* her ideas that were bound to her earth-time survival in the first half of twentieth century America. Attuned to a higher spiritual plane after death, she came to celebrate her granddaughter's freedom struggle, acknowledge her beauty and honor her spiritual path. The grandmother doll was dressed in much the same way her granddaughter of today dresses—and in doing so brought her the gift of acceptance, self-worth and enduring protection—*a blessing.*

"For me, your making my Nana doll was so special. I didn't tell you about Nana, and yet when I opened the box, there she was! She is there for me and now she is always with me on the show. It's important to have her there with me because I know she has my back. That's who she was to me. She's the one who put a love nickel in the palm of my hand when I needed to know "it's okay." She (my Nana doll) has been with me through some

difficult times and I feel Nana's support each time I pass the doll of her sitting in my living room. Thanks for making her for me. Keep at it. Your talent is very unique and you give much to all of us."

—*Hilda*

The Queen

One summer morning in 1998, when I was still living along the New England coast, I happened to meet a couple sitting near me at a cafe. I was hanging up fliers about my doll-making workshop, when one of the women handed me a slip of paper. She advised me to call the woman she called Ms. M, whose number she'd written down for me. She said the woman might be interested in my dolls—and that was all she said. When I got home that afternoon, I decided to call the number. A woman answered. I said I was looking for a Ms. M and explained how and why I had been given her number.

"What kind of dolls do you make? Ms. M asked. We spoke for a time about my doll work.

Before long she asked if I could make a doll for her. I was delighted to do so. I thought like many other times I would make her a doll and perhaps hear back from her once she received it That was as it often happened. Perhaps at some point we'd even connect after that, but not necessarily.

I began work that week and to my surprise the doll's face turned out to be unlike any I had made before. Aside from emerald green eyes, the colors of clay I had been guided to mix turned out to give the appearance of fine, creamy porcelain. The doll's features were delicate, but she had an air of sophistication and power.

When I went to the store to purchase the clothes for her outfit, I ended up being guided by the soul-spirit to the children's section. So, naturally I thought that her healing was something about motherhood. I couldn't have been farther off-base. (So much for the will and mind.) She wanted fabric with reptiles—dinosaurs! Of course, I was aghast at such a request, but not wanting to make yet another trip to the store for not obliging, I purchased the dinosaur fabric.

Then, as I might have guessed, the soul also wanted reptile jewelry. Luckily, I remembered a piece I had in my collection of odd items—a silver lizard wrapped around a large, clear glass marble that I had purchased during one of my many garage sale hunts. With it and her outfit—her Royal Highness emerged. She was a Queen! Not, just any old queen, but Queen of the Reptiles! Literally, I had no idea what it meant or how this woman would react to such a bizarre turn of events.

What the soul-spirit told me was this was her other dimensional self that had been a powerful entity when dinosaurs lived on earth. Her issue was about handling power, which she did well in the present world of leadership, but not in relationships. Apparently, there was someone in her life— a romantic partner, to whom she had given up her power. I knew of women who were very well educated and good in business, but whose confidence and self- worth deteriorated in the presence of domineering men with whom they fell in love. The information that she had been or was, in another dimension, a queen of powerful entities...well, I'd leave that for Ms. M to decide.

Not too long after Ms. M received her doll and the accompanying letter, she called me. She loved the work and we talked a bit about the issue of power. She said that it really meant a lot to her get this message. She mentioned that she was thinking of ending this relationship, as it turned out, and the doll-healing helped her understand what had happened. She didn't mention anything about reptiles. But low and behold, she was in fact a powerful leader and head of a large organization. She invited me to come to the organization's week-long summer conference to talk about my work. My expenses would be covered!

Thus, I was invited to teach about my my doll art at an international writing conference in New York. I met some fascinating women there who would transform my life in ways I could not yet imagine, and one that would eventually lead me on a journey to California. After the first summer, I was invited back to teach my work. I did so for many years. On one such summer, the topic of reptiles came up during the opening oration. The *queen* stood at the podium and asked 500 women writers to be like *reptiles,* with eyes that could move independently from each other—could take in all things, see the bigger picture. As writers and teachers, we were encouraged to broaden our perspective and see deeply. No one else in the audience could have known where that opening line came from. I had to laugh.

Wonders Never Cease

In the fall, as the weather was turning cold again, I began making some dolls for a December holiday doll show. Around the same time I was invited to New York to attend a writing group. I had begun writing about my experience of meeting Mrs. Saxon after attending the writers conference that past summer, where I had been invited to teach a class on doll-making. I was excited about being invited to the writing group and decided I would take some pictures of the dolls along.

One of the dolls for the holiday show was completed and I had already developed the film. She was quite unusual— taller than any doll I had ever made and from a culture I did not know. She had a turquoise band across her head and a silver medallion attached to the front chest area of her garment which was multi-layered turquoise robes. Her skin was a light brown color; her raven black hair was curly, semi-braided and worn long. She was, in a word, stately.

When my closest friend saw this new doll for the first time, she commented on how different this work was from my previous dolls. I decided to ask for some input on a name. I usually did not give names to work that belonged to others, but this doll was for a show, so she needed a name. "Imari," my best friend said. "Call her, *The Goddess, Imari.*"

It was a good name for the doll. So, I put the name on her tag, and added her picture to a little album I usually took with me when I traveled. It was easier to show people what I did, then to tell them. I decided to take the little album with me when I went to the writers' group, the next day.

When I arrived at the New York address it was early evening, and dinner was being served. After a hearty meal everyone had a chance to read a piece of prose or poetry they had written. We went around in a circle. After I read, a woman sitting next to me whom I had just met over dinner—began to read her story. It was a science-fiction piece about a society run by a great female Goddess. The society was in jeopardy of some sort, but my attention was focused on her description of the leader. She described her as a being from an unusually tall race of individuals, with highly developed intuition. She described the leader as a creamy dark-skinned female, wearing a turquoise blue band across the sensitive area of the third eye (her forehead) and a special silver medallion at her chest, over multi-layered robes. As if this description was not enough to make me burst at the seams, she said that the leaders name was... *Imari*. At that point I could barely contain myself.

How could this have happened? What plausible explanation could there be for such a coincidence? I had made a doll, named by my close friend; the name and likeness of a character in a story written by someone who neither of us had ever met. Maybe the Universe was one big joke! Someone up there obviously had a sense of humor. The surprises around every corner never ceased. There was great compassion in the journey on which I had embarked, but the unexpected twists and turns, the levity, the joy— drew me in like a magnet.

⌐⌐

In early spring, I had the opportunity to make a doll for a woman named Carla, who was phobic about snakes and had found a family of them living in a house she had recently bought. Her doll turned out to be a snake charmer, which made total sense. But like all the others healings, I had not known when I began, what it would be.

The snake charmer had a snake in one hand and a flute in the other. A proportionately-sized clay Cobra raised its head from a small ceramic pot that stood in front of the doll. This doll not only represented a past incarnation, but also reflected part of this woman's present character—charming. It was a lesson in the power of what we can bring toward ourselves by thought and action. It was also a lesson about animals in our midst, as symbolic representations and mirrors of our needs, thoughts or fears.

Was it simply an accident that the house contained snakes? The healing pointed to Carla's extreme fear of snakes which had drawn them too her. The doll healing was able to bring Carla new understanding of her power to handle snakes, and her fears. The real snakes finally moved elsewhere of their own accord. After a while, Carla reported, they were no longer a problem. Her phobia also subsided.

I remembered how my doll had at first brought me disturbing dreams and how I had been told that the dreams were lessons in fear. I learned that facing my fears was what had allowed me to move forward, find myself under piles of indoctrination, repudiation and lies. I had uncovered truth now. I had found self-love, Divine Love, joy, humor and healing through creativity—and there was no turning back.

Understanding that fear effects our immune and nervous system, and overall health, facing our fears and beginning to see fear as a teacher of negative energy is the first most important step in healing ourselves.

The Medicine Man

About a year after my first summer conference I was invited to go to California to meet some women who were involved in helping women artists. They had invited several people to hear about my work and afterward several people had ordered dolls. Two of the dolls were ordered as gifts for people who had not been in attendance. Always both helpful and a test of my channeling skills, not having met them would prove fruitful. I might have questioned myself about the first of these dolls had I met the recipient, who I found out later was a fair-skinned blond with blues eyes.

So, I set out to make the first of these dolls. What came was a Native American man. It was clear from soul-spirit that this was a medicine man and everything had to be authentic. I would have to travel to be able to outfit this doll with the proper reverence to his culture. I happened to have planned a trip to see relatives in the Southwest that fall and decided to attend a many nation Powwow, open to the public. I wanted to see the dances and hear the drumming. Because there was also to be sales of Native jewelry, drums and other handmade items, I was excited I might find what I needed for this doll.

I went with a friend and we had an awe-inspiring day. The dance costumes alone took my breath away. I also came home with jewelry, a doll-size drum, deer skin and rabbit fur. While, normally I would have refrained from actual animal products, I knew for this doll authenticity was paramount. After much guidance the doll was done. I was told he was of Blackfoot heritage—and a powerful healer. A heart-filled message came with him directed at the person for whom this doll was intended, apparently a family member.

The recipient was a professional singer, but she had been feeling depressed, soul-spirit advised. She did not see her own value. The message was that she was a healer like him, but it was through her singing voice that she would heal people. When I heard from the woman after she got this gift, she told me her great grandfather was indeed Native American, of Blackfoot heritage. She felt blessed and inspired. The great grandfather doll had given her a new way of understanding her gift and seeing herself in the world.

The Poem

The next doll healing I began at the request of some friends of a another woman, who I had not met. She had been out of town when I had visited to speak at the same gathering. Her friends had ordered it for her as part of her birthday present... what the other part of her present would be, they didn't say. Before I began, a poem started in my head loud and clear. I knew this poem since I'd had to memorize it in junior high school one year. It was by John Mansfield. It started with the line..." *I must go down to the sea again, to the lonely sea and sky. And all I ask is a tall ship and star to steer her by...*"

I loved this poem for some reason, so at first I thought my mind was in charge, not Guidance. Soon though, soul-spirit came in strong. The doll was regal in stature with a commanding aura. She carried with her a deep love of the sea and also a strong connection to her mother whose voice I also detected. It was interesting to me that two strong women came across so powerfully at the same time, each wanting to be heard. The mother, called from spirit wanting fabric associated with her daughter's youth; she had made her child's clothes. The daughter, a woman entering retirement years, needed representation of something regal and formal. I accommodated both of them.

In the doll, through soul-spirit, I could feel a restlessness—a life review she was struggling with as her life was changing. I felt a pull to be back at sea. I found a small doll-size trunk, like a pirates' treasure chest and filled it with maps, crystals, and all sorts of charms that I was guided to add. A small scroll of the entire Mansfield poem I wrote and included as well.

I was to find out that the recipient of the doll was a recently retired career officer in the Navy. So it all made sense. What was the icing on the birthday cake, was that the other part of her gift from her friends, unbeknownst to me till later, was a cruise to Australia. Again I thanked Spirit, but really could not believe the nuances of my gift. How did it all happen was still, after all these years—a miracle.

The Gift of Music

L ike for many spiritual people, the time leading up to 9/11 brought many terrifying dreams. It had been a hard year for me personally, with a loss in my family and home life. Finally, before the actual devastation that was to come, I moved West with family in the summer of 2001. I would not make any healing dolls for another year.

As we all began the healing journey around that time, I decide to write about my work as a healing artist and medium. I had been encouraged by friends all along the way to do so. So I worked as a teacher during the day and stayed up late at night to put stories to paper. I published the first edition of *Artist As Healer* in 2003. I did not know much about publishing. I hired a wonderful young art student, to design the original book and used a local printer. At that time, independent publishing was just beginning.

I found that several people who bought and read the book, ordered dolls. Most people said they were moved by the stories, which pleased me greatly. I never felt like I had chosen this path—it seemed like had chosen me. I have always been of the mind though, that all humans are capable of higher intuitive skills and consciousness. After giving copies away and selling books at conferences and workshops where I taught my craft, I took some time to enter shows.

I entered doll shows on the East and West Coast. One such show was a healing arts conference and show, called

Compassion In Action, where guest speakers included well-known, international healers. They also had a raffle to raise money for charity. The first prize was one of my healing dolls! The second prize was a week-end at famous healing center in the northeast. I was honored to be cast in such company.

Slowly I began to make dolls for clients again. One such doll was for a man, Charles, who was suffering from depression. His partner, Robert had ordered it for him, thinking it might help pull him out of a depression. Charles had recently retired from his career as a therapist and like many people who retire from life-long careers, found himself adrift. Anxiety and depression it seemed were the result of not having a schedule, not feeling needed or just not being able to navigate the aging process. Luckily, he had a home and enough money to not have to worry about basic survival issues. But there was more to his story, as I soon found out.

As soon as I began his doll, I also began to hear music playing, classical music. Everywhere I went I heard Mozart or Beethoven. Violins were particularly a strong component—not surprising to me when I found out that Charles had always loved classical music. He had a large collection of recorded music and a baby grand piano, Robert validated. But Charles found listening to his music saddened him, since his retirement.

Robert had not told me, and I did not know of Charles's treasured violin. However, soul-spirit did and soon his doll, a gentle older man playing a violin and dressed in a fine winter coat and scarf, peered out from twinkling blue eyes. This gentleman and his wife had been kind neighbors, like an uncle and aunt to Charles, when he was a boy. His auntie figure had taught Charles to play the piano and uncle, the old man, played violin duets with Charles after school. He now appeared to come through as a way of letting Charles know that he was very much still with him in spirit and reminded him of the wonderful gift they shared on those afternoons. The old uncle figure was playing his violin for Charles beckoning him to sit at the piano, and play a duet again. Not uncommon to my work was another synchronicity. This gentleman was the same age as Charles was now—sixty-five, when he gave Charles his first music lessons.

I would hear from Charles's partner that the healing doll had performed it's magic. Charles had been overwhelmed with emotion upon receiving it and the message of love and hope along with it. He missed his adopted aunt and uncle. Now their memory turned from loss to joy, knowing they were with him in spirit. Shortly thereafter, Robert purchased season's tickets to the symphony and made a CD of his favorite concertos for a birthday gift. Charles, he reported, was delighted to hear music again. He had begun to play the piano again, as well. He was looking forward to making plans for his new retired life.

Dimensions of the Goddess

Sometime later, I wanted to make a gift of a doll for a new friend, Lupe, as a response to the generosity and kindness she had shown me. She is a retired nurse and an intuitive, herself. She has used her gift for helping people pass over. Aside from tending to others, she loves to travel. She has traveled to many countries and around our own country. Recently however, she has slowed a bit because of a health concern.

In my first attempt to make a doll for her, I felt somewhat hesitant as I tried to open to spirit for a healing. At first I examined my fear. Finding that I was nervous about making a doll for another intuitive, I meditated. Then, I felt much better. I was aware that I had to wait. Sometimes, I was told during meditation to wait and this was one of those times. I trusted Spirit would tell me when the time was right and point the way.

One evening, Lupe invited another friend and I to have dinner at her house and to watch a special TV movie. In the movie, was a woman who had the ability to go between fictitious worlds, from one dimension to another. I watched the movie, but also noticed Lupe as she watched. She seemed to glow. Suddenly, I saw a doll emerging for her. I couldn't wait to get started.

The next day the doll I had envisioned began to appear through the clay as my hands smoothed and sculpted. In the days that followed, I worked at the fine feet adorned in sandals and the long-fingered, strong hands of what was a warrior-Goddess, providing safe passage to the realms. I found a pewter and brass sword, shells, rocks, sequins, satin, velvet and wavy, light auburn locks. She was turning out splendidly.

As I was completing the work, I began hearing a conversation. It was two men talking. Their voices were unsettled and upset. They were talking about some decision of the government that would negatively impact them. All of the sudden, in my peripheral vision I saw a curtain. I looked to my right and the curtain remained …and then opened, as if I was in a theater. Behind the curtain, not more than six feet from me sat a family around a table in a kitchen…the father and son spoke, while the mother served them a meal. The scene was somewhere in Ireland as they spoke with an Irish accent. They were farmers, I was able to ascertain from their dress and surroundings. The time appeared to be before the modern era.

Then, as magically as the vision appeared, it vanished. I sat for a long time replaying the experience in my mind. For many years the voices of Spirit had just been around me when I made a healing… nearby, but not specifically anywhere. Now, just a few yards from me was another dimension where Lupe's ancestors on her mother's side (I would later find out), were sitting and talking about the potato famine that was affecting their lives.

How could that be? I knew now that all time *is* really happening at the same time. I had experienced time overlapping, but not as vividly as this experience. I had created a doll that had brought with it an experience of *quickening* the vibration through the realms. I had sat clearly awake in my seat and peered into another reality right next to me. I was elated, but I knew the time was not yet right to reveal to Lupe all that this powerful healing held. I would know when the time came. And I trusted that she too would remember what she needed to know, in due time. I heard Mrs. Saxon's words and was at peace.

Lupe loved her doll and conversed with it. But I could tell by her stance it would be a while until the doll's real significance would be accepted and Lupe would begin to reap the benefits of the healing. Sometime later, a crisis in Lupe's family would push her to seek further information from me. It would be then that she would allow the door to fully open. I had known to wait. She would not only find healing for her family, but also for herself.

Today Lupe's doll has been moved from its casual spot on a ledge behind the soft chairs in the main room to the bedroom on a table facing the bed. Candles, gold hearts and stars surround the Goddess doll as she stands majestically in a place of importance. Just recently, Lupe spoke to a group of cherished friends, on the occasion of her 73rd birthday.

"I am at peace," she said. "I am not afraid of death. I have been talking to so many on the other side, lately and this world is not all there is…there is vastly more…I want to tell you—so much more, you cannot imagine. My time for traveling here is over. I'm going to spend time contemplating other dimensions of reality."

Creative Changes

In 2006, I went to see a sick relative in Arizona. Since she needed help and there was no one else that could care for her, I ended up spending half the year there. For two more years, I juggled life between California and Arizona. During those years, I mostly painted and taught doll workshops. The desert was an inspiring and healing landscape. I did a bit of writing on a novel I had begun some years before.

When my cousin's health improved, and my grown child was settled in a new job and relationship, I decided it was time for me to think about what I needed. What was foremost on my mind was my up-coming birthday—I would be deciding on partial retirement. I needed a part-time job that would supplement my soon to be retirement income, a new place to call home that was affordable and safe, and a place to finish writing the "great American novel." New friends and community would be the icing on the cake, so to speak.

I had been working on a work of fiction on and off for many years. The story of Anna and her mother that I had begun writing in the 90's was still with me. It had blossomed into an elaborate tale—one I could not have imagined when I began, but one which had ultimately helped me resolve some conflicts in my own life.

I realized that so many of the relationships I'd had with friends, family, and partners had some basis in past life connections. That I dealt with spirits and had visions of actual events in peoples lives, both present and past, made the idea of writing about those connections appealing. What could I gain and how could I share the knowledge I had gleaned over the years in a way that would help others? In deciding to further pursue writing, I had finally accepted myself as a healer. But could I really take on the enormous task of writing a novel?

Suddenly, a idea popped into my head. I had read Jane Robert's novel, "*The Education of Oversoul Seven*" many years before when I was still living in New York. It was a complicated story, but one I resonated with, not realizing at that time —that one day, I would have the gift of creating art that would enable me to access past lives of other people. Now, I had done just that.

I decided I could write something with composites of characters from my experience with people I met as an artist —in a fictitious format. So as the novel began to gel in my mind, I became more intent on moving to a place I could settle down to write. After a few years of holding onto the hope of finding a lucrative job in the city, once I finally resettled full-time in California, I met a woman who lived in Northern California. She invited me to visit her one weekend. I was overjoyed to see the beauty and bounty of the hills, forests and vineyards that spring, when the lush green colors —from lime to viridian, were everywhere. Nature was what I needed, I realized.

Soon I was looking at places 2 hours north of the city, where small towns abound. I found a studio at first, one that would see me through the rest of the summer, and into the following spring. To my absolute joy, I had a family of Angora goats for neighbors on an adjacent farm.

I found a part-time job teaching art at a senior program and every evening I wrote. It was like a dream—the
words just poured out on the page. Fictitious characters
took on a life all their own and often spoke faster than I
could type. The stories I thought I would write, began with
similar themes from some of the doll encounters, then
took off in all directions without my input. Some nights I
would dream of sequences of events, connections between
characters that I had not envisioned or planned— some
would resolve complex issues of time and place that I'd
had difficulty unraveling when I was awake..

During that first year in my new environment, I mostly concentrated on writing and took a break from art. The
following summer, however, I was invited to the home of
a woman named Patricia whose home was in a beautiful setting not far from the center of town. Her property
boasted several large gardens. Filled with blooming trees
and flowers of all kinds, it was like a trip to the botanical
gardens. At the edge of one of the largest gardens where
tomato plants had recently been planted, stood a small
building with a deck that looked out over the expanse of
colorful blooms. The smell of roses, lilies and apple blos-
soms wafted through the air.

I admired the property as she showed me around and
inquired about my art. I had brought some pictures to
show her, so we sat on the little deck as we talked and had
some ice tea. I asked her about the little house. It was one
room with a loft and lots of windows. She said she had
used it as a guest house, but since she had built an exten-
sion on the big house, she had less use for it. Suddenly,
she turned to me. "How would you like to use it for an art
studio?" she asked.

I almost fell off my chair. "Really?" I said. I could not believe her generous offer and my good fortune.

"Oh, that would be more than wonderful! Thank you so much. This is quite amazing! What might be the rent you are considering?" I asked.

She waved her hand and smiled. "No rent, "she said. "I'd be happy to have someone use it—especially an artist like yourself."

I thanked my lucky stars and the angels that brought me such a wonderful surprise. Not long after, I had moved all my art supplies in and began work on a few healing dolls. One was for Patricia. Shortly after I had begun work, I was invited to an International Doll Show—*Play, Power and Healing* at the Petaluma Art Center in Sonoma County, curated by the head of the Psychology Department at SSU. I was thrilled to be part of the growing community of healing artists. Soon, I had made many new friends, was finishing up my first novel that I intended to publish that year, and had plans to teach again at the writers' summer conference on the East coast.

Strength From Trauma

Back again at the writers' conference I met a woman, Sarah, who wanted to have a healing doll. She had lost a family member and was still grieving. As usual, I took her name and birthday and promised that she would hear from me in a month or so with an update.

Arriving home I set to work gathering materials requested by her relative, the soul-spirit who spoke to me from the other side. She wanted a fancy lace trimmed blouse and velvet skirt. She did not want shoes. I was perplexed by the fine outfit and bare feet, so I made her a pair of velvet slippers with little silk flowers. When complete—or so I thought, she requested a rose on her collar. Again, while it did not appeal to me, it was a very strong message, so of course, I obliged.

When I finally stood back and examined my handiwork, I noticed a place on one sleeve that I had failed to complete stitching. I had done some of the finer sewing by hand. A bit in a hurry and also slightly tired at this point, I abruptly raised the arm to be able to fix the issue. The reaction was swift and angry. I was taken back. The soul reacted as if I had actually physically assaulted her. I was shocked. Then came a voice— an explanation. She had been hurt by a close relative. She told me who it had been. I apologized profusely for my abrupt handling, and offered my understanding and sympathy.

This was an unusually intimate moment with a soul-spirit who spoke to me directly from another dimension, about a painful time in her earthly childhood. So, I finished the details, taking my time with delicate care to make sure she was satisfied and soothed.

The following day, I wrote a letter to Sarah to accompany her doll. I wrapped both carefully in bubble wrap, a box, and sent the precious gift to her permanent home. I had not asked the soul any questions, although I could have inquired more in depth about the rose and slippers, but I felt it was enough just to follow the instructions she gave me. I did mention in the letter to Sarah that I was guided by this soul-spirit, (who I now understood was Sarah's sister) to create her in just this way.

Some weeks later, I heard from Sarah. She called to thank me and said she had received the doll of her sister. From her voice I could tell it had been an emotional reunion. She told me the outfit was one her sister had asked to be buried in, and the slippers were what she wore because she had some issues with her feet from birth. The red rose was something their mother had the most unusual experience of receiving from strangers when things were hardest in their lives.

While I had done so many healings by this time, nothing should have surprised me. Still, I was amazed and so grateful that, after all these years, I could still create not only an accurate portrait—but one with so much meaning. I hesitated to ask about the information I had received about the abuse. In one healing that I'd done in the past, I was told by spirit, to keep certain information to myself. (The information I'd been privy to was to enable me to know how to write to the client about her gift for a relative.) So, I ventured to ask indirectly about the sister's confidential communication.

"She asked not to buried near that relative," Sarah said.

"I believe your sister came through to let you know how much she loves you—and to thank you for being there for her." I said a silent prayer and thanked the universe for the gift that made it possible for me to continue to help people.

⤻

After the summer, I concentrated on letting people know about my novel, *Bleed Through*. I had picked the title years before I completed the book. It was a painting term I had learned and a metaphor for how one realm, one dimension *bleeds* into another in my experience. I decided on a pen name, *Ayin Weaver*, to separate my intuitive artist's name from my persona as a writer.

Although I loved learning the craft of writing, I did not think I'd ever write another novel, because it had taken me so many years of hard work. With not much marketing experience, I managed to get some great reviews. One reader said it changed her life! That was my goal—and I was so happy to hear that. I was also delighted that I had accomplished such a feat of endurance! Little did I know that another novel lay in wait for me to write. The next book would lead me on an unexpected journey...an adventure beyond any I had known so far.

Turning Point

2020 altered our reality through the monumental events of the world-wide pandemic. Today, many families are still grieving the death of loved ones. Many around the world are still ill or dying. I feel blessed to be in a land of abundance, where medical advantages are available to save so many lives, including those in my own family.

In the midst of this new time, a change in consciousness is accelerating. Many, young people especially, continue to expand their awareness and attune to higher dimensions. Evident in people around the world waking up and standing up to hate, this new generation promises to bring monumental changes, awakenings and many transformations—as humans enter a new age. Kicking and screaming by some will not prevent the Age of Aquarius from truly taking hold. Humanity is at a turning point.

A turning point in human evolution is an amazing thought, if one considers what evolution means, what possibilities await. That is the message in my writing and one I have received in my own meditation. While I finished and published my second novel, *Souls Of Viridian*, in 2019, before all our lives drastically changed, I continue to share it and hear from people who love it's uplifting message.

Through all the changes, the messages of many healers, light workers, and others who are attuned to listening and opening our minds, hearts and spirits, are acknowledging more and more that we are neither alone in the universe, nor living in one dimension. The universe is multi-dimensional.

And more souls wait in the wings to be heard, to share their love and lighten the load of loved ones who miss them. From my experiences, I believe that there is really no such thing as death—only death of a physical body, not of a soul self.

Earth is like a beautiful school, a place that has the ability, as an entity herself, to vibrate in a slow enough dimension for us to learn lessons as incarnated human beings. We are all called to learn the lessons we need to become empathetic, compassionate, grateful and live in harmony with each other and the earth.

Many believe that before incarnation our souls set an intention, so to speak —lay out a plan, even see it unfold—like a streaming video. Souls in one's soul family agree to participate, each with a set of lessons each wants to learn or in some cases teach other humans. Some lessons are chosen through horrific experiences, in human terms; some through wonderful life-affirming experiences. Our intentional goals and free will are not mutually exclusive—they operate together. Many believe, a soul's destined plan, can be altered by freewill. What I have learned is that a lesson will be learned regardless of the chosen path or deviation from that path, ironically. The universe does have a sense of humor!

As the earth's vibration begins to quicken, time seems to move faster. We are all transcending to a higher level of being, where operating from a place of fear will be replaced by harmony and balance. Fear is powerful, though and is not easily released. Fear that is not life-saving (like running out of a burning building) can be called many things: abuse, jealousy, envy, destruction, cowardliness, anger, victimization, racism, poverty, bullying, discrimination, treachery, greed, hoarding, anxiety, depression...and more.

But trust and love are equally powerful opposites of fear. They allow us to live at a higher vibration of harmony, abundance and peace. Our expanding consciousness, equilibrium and future rest with all of us embracing love, and learning that no matter our physical appearance, gender, identity, origin, abilities, gifts, mates, race, or religious beliefs—*this time around*—we are forever part of a greater universe of beings. And we are all One.

So dear reader—meditate, eat well, rest, love, paint, dance, sing, and laugh...*and open your heart to miracles!*

✑

"Row, row, row your boat, gently down the stream. Merrily, merrily, merrily, life is but a dream."

ע

About the Author

Nina Ayin Reimer began her career in the early 1970s as a medical illustrator (*Our Bodies, Ourselves;* by BWHBC; Simon &Schuster, publisher.) Her background includes many years as an artist and teacher of English, art and health in both the public and private sector. In 1998, she developed her intuitive healing work as *Dolls for the Soul*™. With continued interest in healing, she received her Usui Reiki Masters Certification at the Zen Center in San Francisco in 2004. Over the last 25 years, her healing doll art has been in national doll magazines, newspaper articles, international juried exhibitions, on radio interviews and at major charity fundraising events.

Artist As Healer is Nina Ayin's first nonfiction book originally published in 2003. Out of print for several years, this is the updated edition and reprint. In 2013, she wrote (under her pen name Ayin Weaver) and published her first novel, *Bleed Through,* based on her art of expanding consciousness and understanding of the absurdity of prejudice. In 2019, *Souls of Viridian,* her second novel was published, which took her story of soul connections among diverse characters to the next level.

Nina Ayin lives in California, where a retrospective doll art show, a screenplay and third novel are her current projects.

Made in the USA
Middletown, DE
30 October 2022